£8.99

Learning to Pass

New CLAiT 2006

e creation

SOUTHAMPTON
CITY COLLEGE
LEARNING CENTRE

Unit 6

Ruksana Patel

www.heinemann.co.uk

✓ Free online support
✓ Useful weblinks
✓ 24 hour online ordering

01865 888058

Heinemann

Inspiring generations

Heinemann Educational Publishers
Halley Court, Jordan Hill, Oxford OX2 8EJ
Part of Harcourt Education

Heinemann is the registered trademark of
Harcourt Education Limited

© Ruksana Patel, 2006

First published 2006

10 09 08 07 06 05
10 9 8 7 6 5 4 3 2 1

British Library Cataloguing in Publication Data is available from the British
Library on request.

10-digit ISBN: 0 43508267 1
13-digit ISBN: 978 0 435 082 67 3

Typeset by TechType, Abingdon, Oxon

Original illustrations © Harcourt Education Limited, 2005

Cover design by Wooden Ark Studio
Printed in the UK by Bath Colourbooks

Cover photo © Getty images
Figure 6.49 ©: Stock Photo.com/Lee Dot
Figure 6.50 ©: Stock Photo.com/Heidi Kristensen

Acknowledgements
Every effort has been made to contact copyright holders of material
reproduced in this book. Any omissions will be rectified in subsequent
printings if notice is given to the publishers.

The author would like to thank Abdul Patel for working through the books and
proofs and for his support, patience and valuable feedback during the writing
of this series. Thank you to Stephe Cove for working through this book in
several versions of Photoshop and for his invaluable feedback. Thank you to
Fayaz and Fozia Roked, Penny and Brian Hill for their support. Thank you to
Lewis Birchon and Nick Starren for their valuable input which has improved
the quality of the book and for their constant support, advice and patience
during the production process.

Adobe product screenshots reprinted with permission from Adobe Systems
Incorporated.

Microsoft product screenshots reprinted with permission from Microsoft
Corporation.

Contents

Guidelines for preparing your user area, using ruler guides and downloading images from a digital camera as well as the Definition of terms and General assessment guidelines can be found on the accompanying CD-ROM.

UNIT 6: e-image creation

This book has been designed to cover the syllabus for Unit 6: e-image creation of the OCR Level 1 Certificate/Diploma for IT Users (New CLAiT).

Learning outcomes for Unit 6: e-image creation

A candidate following a programme of learning leading to this unit will be able to:

- identify and use appropriate software correctly in accordance with laws and guidelines
- use basic file handling techniques for the software
- download digital pictures from a digital camera
- import, crop and resize images
- enter, amend and resize text
- manipulate and format page items
- manage and print artwork.

Structure of the qualification

UNIT STATUS	UNIT TITLE
Core unit	Unit 1: File management and e-document production
Optional units	Unit 2: Creating spreadsheets and graphs
	Unit 3: Database manipulation
	Unit 4: e-publication creation
	Unit 5: Create an e-presentation
	Unit 6: e-image creation
	Unit 7: Web page creation
	Unit 8: Online communication
	Unit 9: Computing fundamentals (IC3)
	Unit 10: Key applications (IC3)
	Unit 11: Living online (IC3)

All units are equally weighted. Candidates may work towards the units in any particular order.

Guided learning hours

An average candidate should take around 20 guided learning hours per unit to acquire the knowledge, understanding and skills necessary to pass a unit. However this figure is for guidance only and will vary depending on individual candidates and the mode of learning.

Assessment

Units 1 to 8 are assessed in a centre by a centre assessor and are then externally moderated by an OCR examiner-moderator. OCR sets the assessments. Candidates are allowed a notional duration of $2\frac{1}{2}$ hours for each assessment. If candidates do not pass at the first attempt, they may have other attempts at a unit using a different OCR-set assignment. In order to achieve New CLAiT, candidates must make no critical errors and no more than four accuracy errors. For detailed marking criteria please refer to the OCR Level 1 Certificate/Diploma for IT Users (New CLAiT) Tutor's Handbook.

Certification

Candidates may achieve individual unit certificates, an OCR Level 1 Certificate for IT Users (New CLAiT) or an OCR Level 1 Diploma for IT Users (New CLAiT). Each unit is regarded as a worthwhile achievement in its own right. Candidates have the option of achieving as many or as few units as are appropriate. Candidates will be awarded a unit certificate for each individual unit achieved.

To achieve the Level 1 Certificate for IT Users qualification, candidates are required to achieve three units including the core unit (Unit 1). Candidates who achieve five units, including the core unit (Unit 1), will be awarded an OCR Level 1 Diploma for IT Users (New CLAiT).

Progression

Candidates who are successful in achieving accreditation at Level 1 will be able to progress to the OCR Level 2 Certificate/Diploma for IT Users. New CLAiT also provides a basis for progression to the NVQs which form part of the ITQ suite, NVQ Levels 1, 2 and 3 for IT Users.

Introduction to *ITQ*

The ITQ qualification

The ITQ is a flexible IT user qualification and training package that can be tailored to ensure you are trained in the IT skills that you need for your job. The ITQ is the new NVQ for IT Users. It forms part of the new Apprenticeship Framework for IT Users and it has been bench-marked against the e-skills National Occupational Standards.

New CLAiT 2006 and the ITQ

New CLAiT 2006 can contribute towards the ITQ qualification and the table below shows how New CLAiT 2006 maps against the ITQ. All required ITQ knowledge and skills content are covered in the New CLAiT 2006 units and the CLAiT assessment fully meets the requirements of the assessment strategy for the e-skills UK qualification.

E-SKILLS UK UNIT	NEW CLAIT 2006 UNIT
Operate a computer 1 (OPU1)	Unit 1 File management and e-document production
Word processing 1 (WP1)	Unit 4 e-publication creation
Spreadsheet software 1 (SS1)	Unit 2 Creating spreadsheets and graphs
Database software 1 (DB1)	Unit 3 Database manipulation
Email 1 (MAIL1)	Unit 8 Online communication
Presentation software (PS1)	Unit 5 Create an e-presentation
Website software 1 (WEB1)	Unit 7 Web page creation
Artwork and imaging software 1 (ART1)	Unit 6 e-image creation

This book covers the syllabus for Unit ART1: Artwork and imaging software of the ITQ at Level 1. You can use other units from New CLAiT 2006 and CLAiT Plus 2006 (which are published in Heinemann's *Learning to Pass New CLAiT/CLAiT Plus 2006* series) as well as other qualifications to count towards your ITQ.

Therefore, if you are embarking on the ITQ and you have selected this unit then this book will ensure that you have the knowledge and skills required to successfully complete the unit.

The ITQ Calculator and e-skills Passport

The ITQ can be achieved at three levels and each of the units has points allocated to them so all the units together should add up to the total necessary for the level required. The table below gives you the unit values so that you can see how an ITQ can be built for the level you are aiming to achieve. You can take units from different levels in order to achieve the desired number of points. However, if you aim to achieve the ITQ then you must take the mandatory unit (Make selective use of IT) and at least 60% of your unit choices must be at the ITQ level that you wish to achieve.

e-skills UK has created the e-skills Passport, an online tool, which helps you build your IT user skills profile. It is not a qualification, nor is it a formal appraisal system, but it is a means to steer you towards the right mix of training and/or qualifications that suit you and your employer. For more information visit the e-skills UK website (www.e-skills.com).

	ITQ LEVELS		
	Level 1	Level 2	Level 3
Total required	40	100	180
Total of points to come from optional units at level of qualification	15	40	75

Who this book is suitable for

This book is suitable for:

- candidates working towards: OCR Level 1 Certificate or Diploma for IT Users (New CLAiT), and OCR ITQ qualification
- complete beginners, with no prior knowledge of Photoshop
- use as a self-study workbook – the user should work through the book from start to finish
- tutor-assisted workshops or tutor-led groups
- individuals wanting to learn to use Adobe Photoshop. Default settings are assumed.

Although this book is based on Adobe Photoshop CS (Version 8), it has been worked in Photoshop versions 6, 7 and 9 and Photoshop Elements 2 and has been found to be suitable. Note that a few of the skills will be slightly different and some screen prints will not be identical.

UNIT 6: e-image creation

How to use this book

In Unit 6 you will need to create artwork that contains text, shapes and images. For this you will need to manipulate images, insert and format text and draw shapes. The artwork must be printed in colour. You will also need access to an image that has been taken using a digital camera and to change the resolution of a provided image.

This book is divided into 3 sections:

○ in Section 1 you will learn to use Photoshop, understand file formats, understand resolution, understand and use layers, select colours and insert and format text

○ in Section 2 you will learn how to insert and manipulate images (resize, rotate, flip and crop) and create a variety of shapes

○ in Section 3 you will learn how to amend text, copy items, change the resolution of images and download and work with digital images in Photoshop.

You will use a software program called Adobe Photoshop. Photoshop is an effective computer art program that can be used to create artwork and to make adjustments to images.

What does it mean?

Artwork
The file you will create using images, text and shapes. A finished piece of artwork is also sometimes referred to as an image.

Image
A picture that you may insert into your artwork or that you may make changes to (e.g. change the resolution) or a digital photograph.

How to work through this book

1 Before you begin this unit, make sure that you feel confident with the basics of using a computer and Windows XP. These skills are covered in Chapter 1 of the Unit 1 book *Learning to Pass New CLAiT: File management and e-document production*.

2 Read the explanation of a term first.

3 If there are terms that you do not understand, refer to the **Definition of terms** on the CD-ROM.

4 Work through the book in sequence so that one skill is understood before moving on to the next. This ensures thorough understanding of the topic and prevents unnecessary mistakes.

5 Read the **▸▸ How to...** guidelines which give step-by-step instructions for each skill. Do not attempt to work through them. Read through each point and look at the screenshots. Make sure that you understand all the instructions before moving on.

6 To make sure that you have understood how to perform a skill, work through the **Check your understanding** task that follows. You should refer to the **How to...** guidelines when doing the task.

7 At the end of each section is an Assess your skills table. This lists the skills that you will have practised by working through each section. Look at each item listed to help you decide whether you are confident that you can perform each skill.

8 Towards the end of the book are **Quick reference** guides, **Build-up** and **Practice tasks**. Work through each of the tasks. If you need help, you may refer to the How to… guidelines or Quick reference guides whilst doing the Build-up tasks. Whilst working on the Practice task, you should feel confident enough to use only the Quick reference guides if you need support. These guides may also be used during an assessment.

A CD-ROM accompanies this book. On it are the files that you will need for the tasks. Instructions for copying the files are given below. The solutions for all the tasks can be found on the CD-ROM in a folder called **workedcopies_imgcreation**.

Note: There are many ways of performing the skills covered in this book. This book will provide How to… guidelines that have proven to be easily understood by learners.

Files for this book

To work through the tasks in this book you will need the files from the folder called **files_imgcreation**, which you will find on the CD-ROM that accompanies this book. Copy this folder into your user area before you begin.

 **How to...**   *copy the folder files_imgcreation from the CD-ROM*

Make sure the computer is switched on and the desktop screen is displayed.

1 Insert the CD-ROM into the CD-ROM drive of your computer.

2 Close any windows that may open.

3 On the desktop double-click on the **My Computer** icon.

4 The **My Computer** window is displayed.

5 Under **Devices with Removable Storage** double-click on the CD-ROM drive icon to view the contents of the CD-ROM.

6 A window displaying the contents of the CD-ROM opens.

7 Double-click on the folder **L1_Unit6_ImgCreation**.

FIGURE 1 The **L1_Unit6_ImgCreation** window

8 The **L1_Unit6_ImgCreation** window is displayed.

9 Click on the folder **files_imgcreation**.

10 The folder will be highlighted (usually blue).

11 In the **File and Folder Tasks** section, click on **Copy this folder** (Figure 1).

12 A **Copy Items** dialogue box is displayed (Figure 2).

13 Click on the user area where you want to copy the folder **files_imgcreation**.

14 Click on **Copy**.

15 The folder **files_imgcreation** will be copied to your user area.

16 It is advisable to copy and paste a second copy to another folder in your user area as backup.

Refer to the handout Preparing your work area on the accompanying CD-ROM.

FIGURE 2 **Copy Items** dialogue box

What does it mean?

User area
The workspace on a computer where you will save your files.

One example of a user area is a folder called **My Documents**, Windows XP automatically creates this area. In a centre, you may be given a work area on a network. This area may have a drive name, e.g. G drive. Alternatively, you may save your work on a floppy disk, which is usually the A drive. On your own personal computer, your user area may be in the My Documents folder.

Mouse techniques used in this book

Unless otherwise instructed, always click using the left mouse button.

MOUSE ACTION	DESCRIPTION
Click	Press and release the left mouse button once.
Double-click	Quickly press the left mouse button twice, then release it.
Right-click	Press the right mouse button once, a menu displays.
Hover	Position the mouse pointer over an icon or menu item and pause, a Tool tip or a further menu item will display.
Click and drag	Click with the left mouse button, hold the mouse button down and move the pointer to another location, release the mouse button.

Mouse techniques

In this section you will learn how to:

- understand colour modes and image file formats
- start Photoshop and restore the Photoshop settings
- understand the Photoshop window
- use the Toolbox tools and display and select hidden tools
- display, close and reset palettes
- understand resolution
- create new artwork
- set the orientation
- view the artwork or image on screen
- save artwork as a Photoshop file
- select foreground colour
- save an updated file
- understand layers
- insert, rename, move and delete layers
- insert text
- highlight and format text
- move an item
- close a file
- exit Photoshop.

Understanding colour modes

In Photoshop, colours are set up in **colour modes**. A colour mode determines how colours look on a computer screen and on printouts. You will only need to use **RGB colours**.

The **RGB colour mode** is based on the colours **R**ed, **G**reen and **B**lue – all colours are made up of different amounts of red, green and blue. Computer monitors and TV screens display colours in RGB.

Understanding image file formats

Images can be saved in many different file formats. The table on the next page shows what some of the common file formats stand for.

FORMAT NAME	WHAT IT STANDS FOR
gif	**g**raphics **i**nterchange **f**ormat
jpg / jpeg	**j**oint **p**hotographic **e**xperts **g**roup
psd	**p**hoto**s**hop **d**atafile
bmp	**b**it**m**a**p**
tiff	**t**agged **i**mage **f**ile **f**ormat
pct	Macintosh **pic**ture file

Types of image format

The two most common file formats for images are gif and jpg (also referred to as jpeg).

Gif images are based on 256 colours and are made up of **pixels**. Jpg images are based on 16 million colours. These are compressed and are used for photographs.

A **vector graphic** is based on mathematical formulae and measurements that represent lines and curves. A vector graphic can be reduced or enlarged without losing any detail. Company logos and clip art are examples of vector graphics.

A **bitmap graphic** is a collection of tiny pixels. Bitmaps make it possible to represent almost any combination of colours. Bitmaps lose some of their quality when they are reduced or enlarged.

Photoshop files are saved in psd format. This format preserves all the different parts that make up an artwork as separate layers.

What does it mean?

Pixel
A pixel is simply a dot or tiny coloured square. Each separate dot of colour in an image is a pixel. A collection of thousands of pixels forms an image.

Starting Photoshop

▶▶ How to... *start Photoshop*

1 On the desktop, click on **Start**.
2 The **Windows XP Start** menu is displayed.
3 Click on **All Programs**.
4 The **All Programs** menu appears.
5 Click on **Adobe Photoshop CS**.
6 A **Welcome Screen** may display. Click on **Close**.

Check your understanding *Start Photoshop*

1 Start Photoshop.
2 Compare your Photoshop screen to Figure 6.3 (page 7).
3 If they are not the same refer to 'Is your Photoshop screen different?' on page 6.

Is your Photoshop screen different?

Unlike other computer programs, Photoshop retains the settings used by the previous computer user. Consequently, your screen may look different to Figure 6.3. This is not a problem as you can simply select the options you require and display the windows you need. However, you can restore the default settings in Photoshop easily. Whilst you are becoming familiar with the program you are advised to restore the settings every time you load Photoshop.

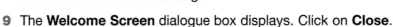

▶▶ How to... *restore the Photoshop settings (optional)*

The default settings can be restored when starting Photoshop through the **Start** menu (but not by using shortcuts on the desktop or Taskbar). If Photoshop is open, close it (click on the **File** menu, click on **Exit**).

1 Click on **Start**.

2 Click on **All Programs**.

3 Click on **Adobe Photoshop CS**. Hold down the **Ctrl** + **Alt** + **Shift** keys **at the same time** whilst the program is loading.

4 A dialogue box will display (Figure 6.1).

5 Click on **Yes**.

6 Another dialogue box will display (Figure 6.2).

7 Click on **No**.

8 Photoshop will open with all windows and options restored to the default settings.

9 The **Welcome Screen** dialogue box displays. Click on **Close**.

FIGURE 6.1 The **Delete Photoshop Settings File** dialogue box

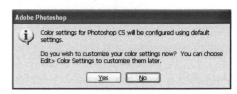

FIGURE 6.2 The **Customize Color Settings** dialogue box

Check your understanding *Start Photoshop and restore the default settings (optional)*

1 Click on the **File** menu. Click on **Exit** to close Photoshop.

2 Load Photoshop through the **Start**, **All Programs** menu. As soon as you click on **Adobe Photoshop CS** hold down the **Ctrl** + **Alt** + **Shift** keys.

3 When the dialogue box displays prompting you to delete the settings file click on **Yes**.

4 If the dialogue box displays asking you to customise the colour settings click on **No**.

5 If Figure 6.1 does not display, close Photoshop and try again.

6 Your screen should look similar to Figure 6.3.

Getting familiar with the Photoshop window

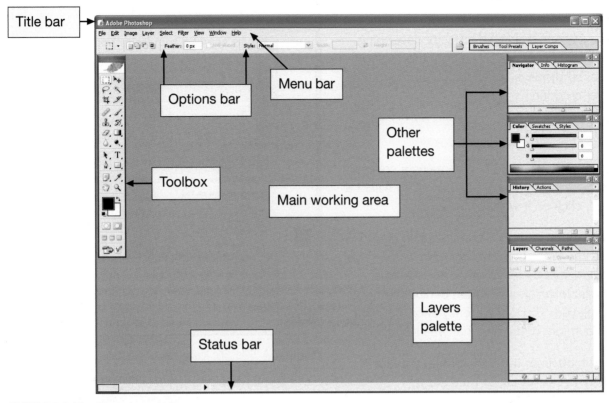

FIGURE 6.3 The Photoshop window

Take a few minutes to learn about the Photoshop screen.

PART OF WINDOW	DESCRIPTION
Title bar	Displays the name of the program and, if an image is maximised, displays the name of the image, which layer is selected and the size of the image on screen (e.g. 100% is the actual size).
Menu bar	A list of options – click on a menu item to see the drop-down menu.
Options bar	Displays options that relate to the tool that is selected in the Toolbox.
Toolbox	Has a variety of tools that allow you to manipulate artwork and images.
Palettes	**Navigator palette:** Displays a miniature of the current image. **Color palette:** Allows you to select colours and patterns. **History palette:** Allows you to undo actions.
Layers palette	A window that allows you to see all the individual layers (items) that make up a piece of artwork.
Main working area	Any open image(s) and artwork will be displayed here. The image(s) can be displayed in a box in the main working area, with the image title bar displayed below the Options bar, or it can be maximised, with the image filename displayed on the Title bar.
Status bar	Displays information about an open image (e.g. the file size, the zoom size).

The Photoshop window

Understanding the Photoshop window

The Options bar is underneath the Menu bar. The options displayed will vary depending on which tool is selected from the Toolbox. A Tool tip displays when you hover the mouse over an option.

Using the Toolbox tools

The Toolbox (Figure 6.4) contains a selection of tools for manipulating images. To select a tool, click on it with the mouse.

Notice that some tools have a little black triangle in the bottom-right corner . This means that there are other related tools available which are hidden behind the one displayed. The tool currently showing is the default tool or the one that was last used.

The tools from the Toolbox that you are likely to use for Level 1 are shown in Figure 6.5. You do not need to memorise these, as a Tool tip will display when you hover your mouse pointer over them.

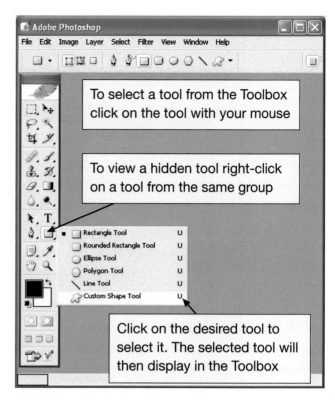

To select a tool from the Toolbox click on the tool with your mouse

To view a hidden tool right-click on a tool from the same group

Click on the desired tool to select it. The selected tool will then display in the Toolbox

FIGURE 6.4 Selecting tools from the Toolbox

>> **How to...** *display and select hidden tools*

1 Right-click anywhere on a tool in the **Toolbox**.

2 The related hidden tools will be displayed. A black square dot to the left of the tool shows which one is currently selected (Figure 6.4).

3 Click on a tool to select it.

4 The tool you selected will now display on the **Toolbox**.

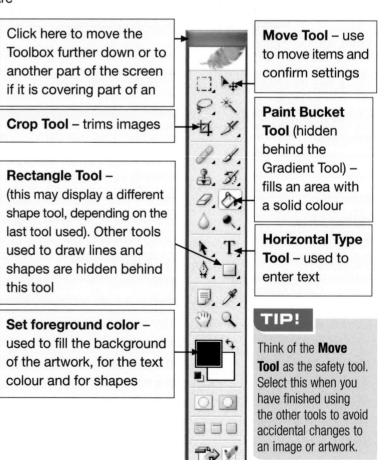

Click here to move the Toolbox further down or to another part of the screen if it is covering part of an

Crop Tool – trims images

Rectangle Tool – (this may display a different shape tool, depending on the last tool used). Other tools used to draw lines and shapes are hidden behind this tool

Set foreground color – used to fill the background of the artwork, for the text colour and for shapes

Move Tool – use to move items and confirm settings

Paint Bucket Tool (hidden behind the Gradient Tool) – fills an area with a solid colour

Horizontal Type Tool – used to enter text

TIP!

Think of the **Move Tool** as the safety tool. Select this when you have finished using the other tools to avoid accidental changes to an image or artwork.

FIGURE 6.5 The basic Toolbox tools suitable for Level 1 users

1 Hover with your mouse over some of the tools in the **Toolbox**. Locate the following: **Move Tool, Crop Tool, Horizontal Type Tool, Rectangle Tool, Gradient Tool**.

2 Select the **Move Tool** ⊹. Look at the options available on the **Options bar**.

3 Select the **Crop Tool** ⊐. Look at the options available on the **Options bar**. Notice that these options have now changed.

4 Select the **Rectangle Tool** ☐. Notice the different options in the **Options bar**.

5 The **Rectangle Tool** has a little black triangle in the corner. Right-click on this tool and select the **Line Tool** ⟍. The **Line Tool** should now be displayed in the **Toolbox**.

6 Select the **Horizontal Type Tool** T. Notice the different options in the **Options bar**. From these options the font type, font size, colour, etc. can be selected.

7 Right-click on the **Gradient Tool** ▇ and select the **Paint Bucket Tool** ◇.

8 Select the **Move Tool** again.

Understanding palettes

Palettes are windows that include a variety of options. They are usually displayed on the right-hand side of the screen. To make the screen less crowded, you are advised to close palettes which you are unlikely to use. Keep only the Layers palette open when you are working on the artwork.

▶▶ How to... *display palettes*

1 Click on the **Window** menu.

2 Click on the palette required, e.g. **Layers**.

3 Any palette that is already displayed will have a tick displayed to the left of it in the menu.

▶▶ How to... *close palettes*

Click on the red cross ✖ at the top-right corner of the palette window.

TIP!

To reset the palettes to their original places, click on the **Window** menu, click on **Workspace**, click on **Reset Palette Locations**.

1 Close the **Navigator**, **Color** and **History** palettes.

2 Click on the blue bar at the top of the **Layers** palette. Practise dragging this palette further up and down.

Understanding resolution

The resolution of an image is determined by the number of **pixels per centimetre** or **pixels per inch** (**ppi**) printed on a page. In Photoshop you can easily change the resolution of an existing image and select an appropriate resolution for a new piece of artwork.

An image with a high resolution contains more, and therefore smaller, pixels than an image with a low resolution. Higher-resolution images can reproduce more detail and subtler colour changes than lower-resolution images because the pixels are packed more tightly (the density of the pixels is greater). A higher resolution will produce a better quality image but the file size will be larger.

Reducing the print resolution of an image makes each pixel larger, which results in **pixilation** – a printout with larger, coarse-looking pixels (the individual squares are more obvious).

In an OCR assignment the resolution for the artwork to be created will not be specified, you may select any resolution. 28.346 pixels/cm (72 pixels/inch) is the standard resolution of computer screens and produces a reasonable-quality image. A slightly higher resolution of between 60 and 78 pixels/cm will produce a better-quality image.

> **TIP!**
>
> The higher the resolution of the artwork the better the quality of the image but the larger the file size.

Creating artwork

▶▶ How to... *create a new artwork*

1 Click on the **File** menu.

2 Click on **New**.

3 The **New** dialogue box will open (Figure 6.6).

4 Click in the **Name** box, delete the existing text and enter the required name.

5 Click on the drop-down arrow to the right of the **Width** box and select **cm. cm** should display to the right of the **Height** box as well.

6 Click in the **Width** box. Delete any contents and enter the required width.

7 Click in the **Height** box. Delete any contents and enter the required height.

8 Click on the drop-down arrow to the right of the **Resolution** box and select **pixels/cm**.

9 Click in the **Resolution** box. Delete any contents and enter the required resolution.

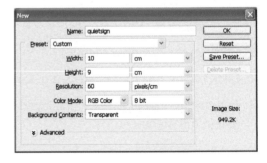

FIGURE 6.6 Creating new artwork

> **TIP!**
>
> Select cm for the **Width** and **Height** and pixels/cm for the **Resolution** BEFORE you enter the numbers in these boxes.

10 Click on the drop-down arrow to the right of the **Color Mode** box and select **RGB Color**.

11 Click on the drop-down arrow to the right of **Background Contents** and select **Transparent**.

12 Check that all the above settings are correct.

13 Click on **OK**.

▶▶ How to... *set the orientation*

1 Click on the **File** menu.

2 Click on **Page Setup**.

3 The **Page Setup** dialogue box will be displayed.

4 Click on the button for **Portrait** or **Landscape**.

5 Click on **OK**.

Check your understanding *Create new artwork*

1 Create a new piece of artwork as follows:

Name:	**quietsign**
Width:	**10 cm**
Height:	**9 cm**
Resolution:	**60 pixels/cm**
Mode:	**RGB color**
Contents:	**Transparent**

2 Notice that a new layer has been created automatically in the **Layers** palette.

3 Set the page orientation to **Portrait**.

TIP!

To undo an action: click on the **Edit** menu then click on **Step Backward**.

To undo one step at a time: hold down **Ctrl + Alt** and tap the **Z** key.

Transparent backgrounds in Photoshop

In Photoshop, a transparent background displays as grey and white squares on the screen (see Figure 6.7). It is good practice to select a transparent background when you create a new artwork, so the background can be filled with any colour and this colour can be changed easily.

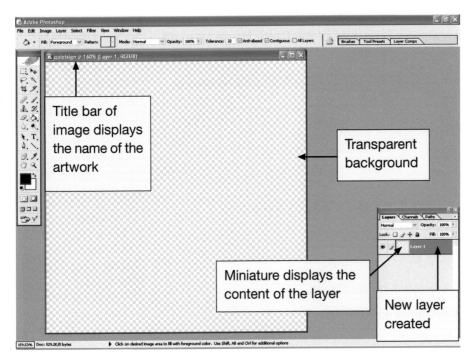

FIGURE 6.7 A transparent background displays on screen as a grey and white checkerboard in Photoshop

Viewing artwork or an image on screen

The size that your artwork or image appears on the screen is not necessarily the size of your image. While working on your artwork or image it is clearer if the entire picture is displayed as large as the computer screen will allow.

▶▶ How to... *view the artwork or image on screen*

1 To see the size of the artwork or image when it will be printed, click on the **View** menu. Click on **Print Size**.

2 To view the whole image clearly, click on the **View** menu. Click on **Fit on Screen**.

3 To **zoom in** on the artwork or an image, hold down the **Ctrl** key and tap the + key. You will zoom in every time you tap the + key.

4 To **zoom out**, hold down the **Ctrl** key and tap the - key.

Saving the artwork

You must make sure that you save your artwork in the appropriate file format. While you are still working on the artwork you should save it in Photoshop file format. This is because, even though the file sizes are larger, they preserve all the layers, so you will be able to edit any items in your artwork easily. When you have completed the final artwork it can then also be saved in other file formats, e.g. jpg or gif, which have smaller file sizes but only have one layer. Saving as jpg and gif is covered in Section 3.

TIP!

To save into a new folder, first create the folder by clicking on the **Create New Folder** icon. Enter a name for the new folder and then double-click on the folder to open it.

▶▶ How to... save artwork as a Photoshop file

1 Click on the **File** menu.

2 Click on **Save As**.

3 The **Save As** dialogue box displays.

4 Click on the drop-down arrow to the right of the **Save in** box and double-click to open the folder where you want to save your file.

5 In the **File name** box enter the required filename (this may already be displayed if you have given your new artwork a name).

6 In the **Format** box make sure that **Photoshop (*.PSD,*.PDD)** is selected.

7 In the **Save Options** section check that the **Layers** box is ticked (Figure 6.8).

8 Click on **Save**.

9 A **Photoshop Format Options** dialogue box may display. Click on **OK**.

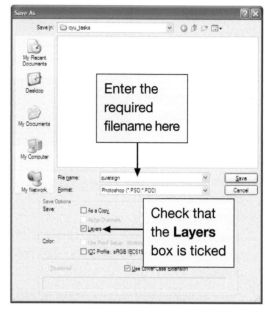

Enter the required filename here

Check that the **Layers** box is ticked

FIGURE 6.8 Saving as a Photoshop file

Check your understanding *View your artwork and save*

1 **Zoom in** on the artwork to approximately 300% (the title bar and the status bar will display the zoom percentage).

2 Now **zoom out** to approximately 33%.

3 Use the **View** menu to view the **print size** of your artwork.

4 Use the **View** menu to set the view to **fit** the artwork **on screen**.

5 Save the artwork as a Photoshop file using the filename **quietsign**

Selecting colours

You will need to select colours for the artwork's background, for shapes and for text. There are various ways to select colours but the simplest is to set the foreground colour from the Toolbox.

▶▶ How to... select a foreground colour

Use this method to select a colour to fill the background of the artwork, to fill a shape with a colour or to select a text colour. Alternatively, for a shape or the text colour, a colour square will display on the **Options bar**. Click in this colour square and the **Color Picker** dialogue box will display.

TIP!

The Paint Bucket Tool uses the colour in the **Set foreground color** box to fill the artwork background NOT the colour set in the **Set background color** box.

1 From the **Toolbox** click in the **Set foreground color** box (Figure 6.5, page 8).

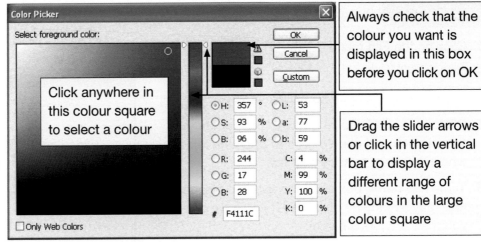

2 The **Color Picker** dialogue box will display (Figure 6.9).

FIGURE 6.9 The **Color Picker** dialogue box

3 Click in the large square to choose a colour from the range displayed or, to view other colours, click in the vertical bar or drag the slider arrows. The large colour square will display a different range of colours.

4 Click in the large colour square to choose a colour.

5 Check that the colour you selected is now displayed in the top rectangle (to the left of the OK button).

6 Click on **OK**.

7 The colour you selected should now be displayed in the **Set foreground color** box on the **Toolbox**.

▶▶ How to... *fill the background of the artwork with a colour*

1 Make sure the colour required is displayed in the **Set foreground color** square in the **Toolbox**.

2 From the **Toolbox**, select the **Paint Bucket Tool** 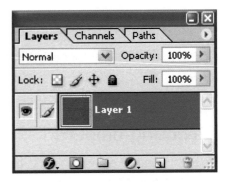.

3 On the **Options bar**, check that **Foreground** Fill: Foreground ▼ is displayed to the right of the Fill box.

4 Move the mouse into the artwork area. The mouse pointer displays as a paint bucket.

FIGURE 6.10 The **Layers** palette

5 Click once.

6 The background of the artwork will be filled.

7 Observe the **Layers** palette. The miniature for the layer now displays the fill colour (Figure 6.10).

TIP!

Once you have used the **Paint Bucket Tool** , click on the **Move Tool** ▶₊ to avoid making any accidental changes to the artwork.

TIP!

When you fill the background of the artwork, the colour that displays in the **Set foreground color** tool on the Toolbox is used as the fill colour.

1 Click on the **File** menu.

2 Click on **Save**, OR press **Ctrl + S**.

Check your understanding Set the foreground colour and fill the background of the artwork

1 In your artwork **quietsign** select **red** as the foreground colour.

2 Using the **Paint Bucket Tool** fill the artwork with red.

3 Check the **Layers** palette. The fill colour should be displayed in the miniature of **Layer 1**.

4 Save the artwork keeping the filename **quietsign**.

Understanding layers

Most of the artwork that you produce in Photoshop will involve using layers. A layer works as a collage – one effect is built upon another to create a final image. All work must have at least one layer (a background layer) and most will have more. The number of layers that you can use is almost unlimited.

Think of layers as sheets of clear plastic – when laid on top of one another all the individual layers make up an entire image, with each layer containing a part of the whole image. It does take a while to get used to working in this way, but it is very effective as you can radically change one layer while leaving the rest of your artwork intact.

The Layers palette shows all the layers that have been used to make the final piece of artwork and you can work with any layer at any time. To select a layer simply click on it in the Layers palette. All the other layers will be unaffected by any changes you may make. An active layer has a paintbrush symbol to the right of the eye symbol and the layer background in the Layers palette is a darker shade, usually blue (Figure 6.12 on page 16).

A layer displaying an eye indicates that the layer will be visible both on the screen and when printed. A blank box instead of an eye indicates that the layer is hidden and will not show, either on the screen or when printed.

It is advisable to have the Layers palette visible when you are working as this allows you to easily select the layer you need. To display the Layers palette: click on the **Window** menu and then click on **Layers.**

Layout sketches

In an OCR assignment you will not be instructed to create layers, as you are expected to know how to use your software. You will be provided with two layout sketches. Layout sketch 1 will show the approximate positioning of items on the original artwork while layout sketch 2 will show the approximate positioning of items on the amended artwork. You must create a new layer for each item (image, text and shape) of the artwork. Examples of layout sketches have been included for use in the tasks in this book. Refer to pages 20, 41, 55, and 60.

▶▶ How to... *insert a new layer*

1 Click on the **Layer** menu.

2 Click on **New**.

3 From the submenu, click on **Layer**.

4 The **New Layer** dialogue box will open.

5 In the **Name** box, enter a suitable name for the layer.

6 Check that the **Color** box displays **None** and that the **Mode** box displays **Normal** (Figure 6.11).

7 Click on **OK**.

8 A new layer will be inserted into the artwork.

9 Look at the **Layers** palette. The new layer should display. The miniature will display the contents of this layer as transparent (grey and white checkerboard) (Figure 6.12).

> **TIP!**
> Before you insert a new layer, check which layer is the active layer because a new layer will be inserted immediately **above** the active layer.

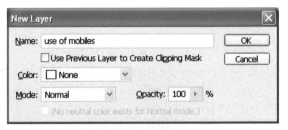

FIGURE 6.11 Inserting a new layer

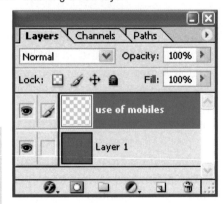

FIGURE 6.12 A new layer in the **Layers** palette

> **TIP!**
> Layer names will not be provided in an OCR task, you should think of a suitable name as this will help you identify each layer's content.

> **TIP!**
> To rename a layer, right-click over the layer name in the layers palette. A menu displays, select **Layer Properties**, in the **Layer Properties** dialogue box, delete the existing name and enter the new layer name, click **OK**.

Check your understanding *Insert a new layer*

1 In your artwork **quietsign**, insert a new layer.

2 Name this layer **use of mobiles**

3 Observe the new layer in the **Layers** palette.

4 Save the updated artwork keeping the filename **quietsign**.

▶▶ How to... *delete a layer*

1 In the **Layers** palette, click on the layer to be deleted.

2 Click on the **Layer** menu.

3 Click on **Delete**.

4 From the submenu, click on **Layer**.

5 A dialogue box displays prompting you to confirm the delete (Figure 6.13).

6 Click on **Yes**.

7 The selected layer and its contents will be deleted.

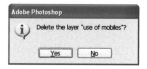

FIGURE 6.13 Deleting a layer

TIP!

Use this method to delete any layers created in error.

Check your understanding *Delete a layer*

1 In your artwork **quietsign**, delete the layer **use of mobiles**

2 Save the updated artwork keeping the same filename.

Inserting text

You will need to insert more than one block of text (phrase) on a piece of artwork using specified text colours.

In Photoshop, text is inserted using the Horizontal Type Tool **T** and the related options on the Options bar (e.g. text size and font name). The text colour can be selected from the Options bar or by setting the foreground colour.

A new layer is inserted automatically when you use the Horizontal Type Tool, the text entered displays as the layer name. You may keep this name or rename the layer.

TIP!

Use the same case as shown. Insert one space between each word. Do not enter a full stop at the end of a line of text.

▶▶ How to... *insert text*

1 Select the text colour by setting the foreground colour. (Refer to 'How to... select a foreground colour' on page 13.)

2 From the **Toolbox**, select the **Horizontal Type Tool**.

3 In the **Options bar**, click on the drop-down arrow to the right of the **Set the font family** box. A list of fonts displays. Click to select a suitable font.

4 Click on the drop-down arrow to the right of the **Set the font size** box. A list of sizes displays. Click to select a suitable font size.

5 Check the colour in the **Set the text color** box is correct. If it is not, click on the box and the **Custom Picker** dialogue box displays. Select a text colour and click on **OK**.

6 Move your mouse into the artwork area and click and drag the mouse to draw a text frame. Make sure you draw the frame to the appropriate width shown on the layout sketch for that block of text.

7 A cursor will display in the text frame. Enter the required text (Figure 6.14). A new layer will be automatically inserted.

8 Do not worry if the text size is not displayed correctly at this point, it can be formatted after it has been entered.

9 Click on the **Move Tool** to deselect the text frame.

TIP!

Select a smaller font size to start with. If the font size is too large to fit within the text frame it will not display on screen.

What does it mean?

Cursor
A flashing vertical line which shows where text will be entered.

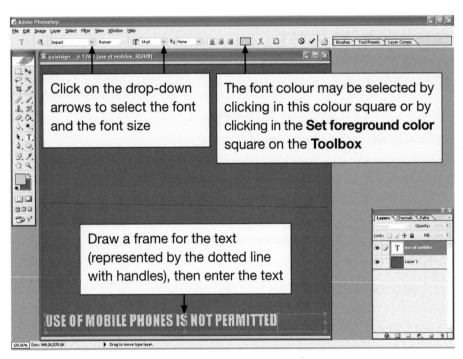

FIGURE 6.14 Adding text to your artwork

Click on the drop-down arrows to select the font and the font size

The font colour may be selected by clicking in this colour square or by clicking in the **Set foreground color** square on the **Toolbox**

Draw a frame for the text (represented by the dotted line with handles), then enter the text

USE OF MOBILE PHONES IS NOT PERMITTED

▶▶ How to... *highlight text*

To format text you will usually need to highlight it.

1 Select the required text layer.

2 Make sure the **Horizontal Type Tool** is selected from the **Toolbox**.

3 Click within the text. The text frame will display with handles.

4 Click and drag the mouse from one end of the text to the other (you can start at the beginning or the end of the text). Alternatively, click at one end of the text, hold the **Shift** key and click at the other end of the text.

TIP!

To highlight a line of text, triple-click in the line.

TIP!

You can only highlight text on one layer at a time. If you have more than one text layer you will need to work on one layer at a time.

▶▶ How to... *format text*

1 Make sure the **Horizontal Type Tool** is selected from the **Toolbox**.

2 Highlight the text.

3 Select the options required on the **Options bar**.

4 To set a font size that is not displayed on the list, click in the **Font Size** box, enter a size (you can use decimal places) T̲ 16.5 ✔ then press **Enter**.

5 When you have formatted the text, click on the **Move Tool** ▶⊕ to deselect the text frame.

▶ How to... *move an item (text, shape or an image)*

1 Make sure the correct layer is selected in the **Layers** palette.

2 From the Toolbox, select the **Move Tool** ▶⊕.

3 Either click and drag the mouse to move the item or hold down the **Ctrl** key and tap the **arrow** key on the keyboard.

▶▶ How to... *close artwork or an image*

1 Click on the **File** menu.

2 Click on **Close.**

▶ How to... *exit Photoshop*

1 Click on the **File** menu.

2 Click on **Exit**.

Note: The layout sketches for the Check your understanding tasks can also be found on the accompanying CD-ROM. Print the page from the CD-ROM so that you can refer to it when doing the tasks.

1   In your artwork **quietsign**, set the foreground colour to **yellow** from the **Toolbox**.

2   From the **Toolbox**, select the **Horizontal Type Tool**.

3   Select a suitable font and font size.

4   Draw a text box at the bottom of the artwork which fits most of the width.

5   Enter the following text on one line:

    USE OF MOBILE PHONES IS NOT PERMITTED

6   Format the text so that it fills most of the width of the artwork as shown in Layout Sketch 1 (Figure 6.15).

7   Move the text so that it is placed at the bottom of the artwork.

8   Make sure all the text remains within the artwork and does not touch any of the edges.

9   Save the artwork keeping the filename **quietsign**.

10 Close the artwork.

11 Exit Photoshop.

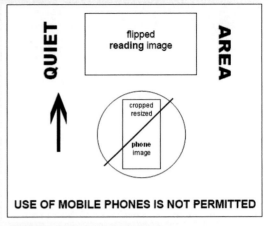

FIGURE 6.15 Layout Sketch 1

ASSESS YOUR SKILLS – Create artwork using layers

By working through Section 1 you will have learnt the skills listed below. Read each item to help you decide how confident you feel about each skill.

- understand colour modes and image file formats
- start Photoshop and restore the Photoshop settings
- understand the Photoshop window
- use the Toolbox tools and display and select hidden tools
- display, close and reset palettes
- understand resolution
- create new artwork
- set the orientation
- view the artwork or image on screen
- save artwork as a Photoshop file
- select foreground colour
- save an updated file
- understand layers
- insert, rename, move and delete layers
- insert text
- highlight and format text
- move an item
- close a file
- exit Photoshop.

If you think you need more practice on any of the skills above, go back and work through the skill(s) again.

If you feel confident, move on to Section 2.

Section 2: Insert images, create shapes and manipulate items (text, images, shapes)

LEARNING OUTCOMES

In this section you will learn how to:

- open existing artwork
- rotate an item
- insert an image into artwork
  - open the image
  - copy an image
  - paste the copied image into the artwork
  - close the original image
- resize an original image and an item on a layer
- flip an item
- crop an image
- create a circle (fixed size and freehand)
- draw a line
- draw custom shapes
- print in colour
- draw a rectangle, a triangle, a star and a starburst.

▶▶ **How to...** *open existing artwork*

1 Click on the **File** menu.
2 Click on **Open**.
3 The **Open** dialogue box will display.
4 Click on the drop-down arrow to the right of the **Look in** box and open the folder (and subfolders) in your user area where the artwork is saved.
5 Click on the name of the artwork.
6 The filename will be highlighted. A miniature displays at the bottom of the **Open** dialogue box.
7 Click on **Open**.

Rotating an item

Rotate means to change the direction of an item (text, image or shape) by a number of degrees. Items can be rotated freely or by a set number of degrees. You will be required to learn how to rotate by 180° and

90° clockwise and 90° anticlockwise. Figure 6.16 shows an original item that has then been rotated by 90° clockwise, 90° anticlockwise and 180°.

Go   **ஃ**   **ஃ**   **oꓯ**

FIGURE 6.16 Examples of rotation

▶▶ How to... *rotate an item (text, image, shape) on a layer in the artwork*

1 Check that the layer containing the item to be rotated is the active layer in the **Layers** palette.

2 Click on the **Edit** menu.

3 Click on **Transform** (this will display as **Transform Path** if the layer contains a drawn shape).

4 Select one of the following options from the submenu:

Rotate 180°, **Rotate 90° CW**, **Rotate 90° CCW** (Figure 6.17)

What does it mean?

CW: Clock**W**ise.
CCW: (Counter **C**lock**W**ise or anticlockwise).

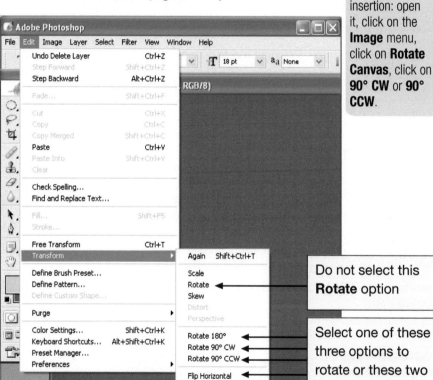

Do not select this **Rotate** option

Select one of these three options to rotate or these two options to flip

FIGURE 6.17 Rotating or flipping and item on a layer

Refer to **Layout Sketch 1** on page 20 or your printed copy.

1. Open your artwork **quietsign**. Check that the top layer is the active layer.

2. Using the **Horizontal Type Tool** enter the text **QUIET** in **yellow**.

3. Check that a new text layer has been created in the **Layers** palette.

4. Rotate the new layer containing the text QUIET **90° anticlockwise** (CCW).

5. Move this text towards the top left of the artwork, as shown in **Layout Sketch 1**.

6. Using the **Horizontal Type Tool** enter the text **AREA** in **yellow**.

7. Check that a new layer has been created in the **Layers** palette.

8. Rotate the text layer containing the text AREA **90° clockwise** (CW).

9. Move this text towards the top right of the artwork, as shown in **Layout Sketch 1**.

10. Save the updated artwork keeping the filename **quietsign**.

> **TIP!**
>
> Always check which layer is the active layer, as a new layer will be inserted ABOVE the active layer.

> **TIP!**
>
> If you make a mistake, click on the **Edit** menu, then click on **Step Backward**.

Inserting images

You will be provided with at least two images to be inserted into the artwork. Images will usually be provided in **gif** and/or **jpg** format. You will also need to manipulate these images (e.g. **crop**, **resize**, **flip**, etc).

In Photoshop, there is a quick way of inserting a jpg image: simply open it and then click and drag it into the artwork. A new layer is created automatically. The second method, described below, is appropriate for all image types.

▶▶ How to... *insert an image into artwork*

Inserting an image into artwork can be done in five stages:

- ○ Create and name a new layer in the artwork.
- ○ Open the image from within Photoshop.
- ○ Select the whole image and copy it.
- ○ Move to the artwork and paste the image into it.
- ○ Close the original image without saving it.

Before you open an image:

1. Create a new layer in the artwork and give the layer a suitable name (e.g. the name of the image).

> **TIP!**
>
> A new layer will be created automatically when you insert an image (even if you do not create it). The advantage of creating and naming a layer first is that it is easier to identify each layer's content.

2 From the **Toolbox**, select the **Move Tool** to avoid making accidental changes to the image (e.g. filling it with colour!).

To open an image:

3 Click on the **File** menu.

4 Click on **Open.**

5 The **Open** dialogue box will display.

6 Click the drop-down arrow to the right of the **Look in** box and open the folder (and subfolders) in your user area where the image is stored.

7 In the **Files of type** box, make sure that **All Formats** is selected.

8 In the main window, click on the name of the image.

9 The image will be highlighted (usually blue) and a miniature of the image will display at the bottom of the **Open** dialogue box (Figure 6.18).

10 Click on **Open.**

11 The image will open in a new window in Photoshop.

FIGURE 6.18 The **Open** dialogue box

To copy an image:

12 Select the image by clicking on its **title bar**.

Note: the **title bar** of the active (selected) file will be a darker shade (usually blue). When you have more than one file open, always check which is the active image.

Note: If you need to crop an image, do so at this stage. Refer to 'How to… crop an image' on page 29.

13 Click on the **Select** menu.

14 Click on **All.**

15 The entire image should be highlighted. A marquee displays around the outside edge of the image.

16 Click on the **Edit** menu.

17 Click on **Copy.**

You will not see any change at this point – the image is now copied into Photoshop's clipboard (its memory).

To paste a copied image into the artwork:

18 Click on the **title bar** of the artwork to make this the active file.

19 In the **Layers** palette, make sure that the new layer is selected.

20 Click on the **Edit** menu.

21 Click on **Paste.**

22 The image will display in the new layer in the artwork.

23 Save the artwork.

TIP!

If the image is partly hidden behind the Toolbox, click and drag the blue bar on the Toolbox to move it further down.

TIP!

If an open image is not visible on screen (it is hidden behind the artwork), click on the **Window** menu. The name of all open files will be listed at the bottom of this menu. Click on the name of the image to bring it to the front.

TIP!

To move an image, click and drag the blue title bar of the image.

What does it mean?

Marquee
A moving dashed line, also known as marching ants!

To close an image that has been inserted:

24 Click on the **title bar** of the image to make this the selected file.

25 Click on the **File** menu.

26 Click on **Close**.

Check your understanding *Insert an image into the artwork*

For this task you will need the image file **reading** from the folder **files_imgcreation**. This file is provided in **jpg** format.

1 In your artwork **quietsign**, insert a new layer using the name **reading image**

2 From within Photoshop, open the image **reading**.

3 Select all of the image then copy it.

4 Move to your artwork **quietsign**. Click on its **title bar** to make the artwork the active file.

5 Paste the image **reading** into the artwork.

6 Do not be concerned if the image is not the correct size or is covering some text. You will learn how to resize images later.

7 Save the artwork keeping the filename **quietsign**.

8 Close the image file **reading**.

Resizing Items

When an item is resized, the whole item is made bigger or smaller. When this happens, you must make sure that you keep the item's original shape. This is referred to as **maintaining the original proportions**.

Look at the examples below:

FIGURE 6.19 Original image

FIGURE 6.20 Original image resized with the original proportions maintained – correct

FIGURE 6.21 Original image resized but now distorted – incorrect

An image can be resized before or after it is inserted into the artwork. However, you are generally advised to do this afterwards. The advantage of this is that you can see by how much you need to resize the image in relation to the artwork, without altering the original image. Also, if you resize before insertion you may still need to resize the image again afterwards if it is still the wrong size.

However, in the case of very large images, you may find it easier to resize before insertion and then make any final adjustments afterwards. This is because some images may be too large to fit in the artwork.

▶▶ How to... *resize an original image*

1 Open the image and make sure it is selected.

2 Click on the **Image** menu.

3 Click on **Image Size**. A dialogue box displays.

4 Make sure there is a tick in the box for **Constrain Proportions**.

5 In the **Document Size** section, enter the new **Width**. Photoshop will automatically change the height whilst maintaining the proportion.

6 Click on **OK**.

▶▶ How to... *resize an item (text, images, shapes) on a layer*

1 In the artwork, check that the layer containing the item to be resized is the active layer in the **Layers** palette.

2 Click on the **Edit** menu.

3 Click on **Transform** (or **Transform Path** if the layer contains a shape).

4 From the submenu, click on **Scale**.

5 The item will be surrounded by a frame with handles (Figure 6.22).

TIP!

To make a layer active, simply click on the layer name in the **Layers** palette.

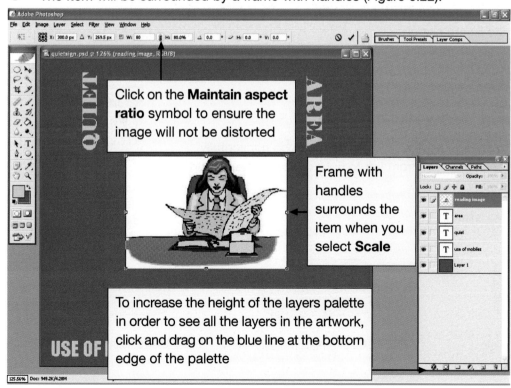

FIGURE 6.22 Resizing an item

6   On the **Options bar**, click on the **Maintain aspect ratio** symbol .
    This will ensure that the original proportions are maintained.

7   Resize the image using one of the following methods:

    ○ click and drag a corner handle

    ○ on the **Options bar**, enter a number in the **W** (Width) box.
      Photoshop will automatically change the **Height** (H). To reduce
      the size, enter a number below 100. To increase the size, enter a
      number above 100. The number you enter is a percentage increase
      or decrease.

8   When you are satisfied with the new size, click on the
    Move Tool ▸⊕.

9   A dialogue box will display (Figure 6.23).

10 Click on **Apply**.

11 Use the **Move Tool** to position the image as required.

FIGURE 6.23 The **Transformation** dialogue box

Check your understanding *Resize and move an image*

1 In your artwork **quietsign**, select the layer **reading image**.

2 Reduce the size of the **reading** image so that it is visibly smaller.

3 Move the image to the top of the artwork between the words **QUIET**
   and **AREA**.

4 Refer to **Layout Sketch 1** on page 20. If necessary, select the
   layers containing the text **QUIET** and **AREA** and position the text as
   shown on the layout sketch.

5 Save the updated artwork keeping the filename **quietsign**.

> **TIP!**
>
> To move an image use
> the **Move Tool** or hold
> down the **Ctrl** key and
> tap the arrow key.
>
> To position an item
> precisely, refer to
> 'Using ruler guides to
> align items' on the CD-
> ROM.

> **TIP!**
>
> To flip an image before
> insertion: open it,
> click on the **Image**
> menu, click on **Rotate
> Canvas**, click on **Flip
> Horizontal** or **Flip
> Vertical**.

Flipping items

To **flip** an item is to change its direction. An item can be horizontally
flipped (the direction is changed from left to right or vice versa) or vertically
flipped (it is turned upside down).

Look at the following examples:

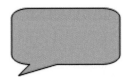

FIGURE 6.24 Original item

FIGURE 6.25 Item flipped horizontally

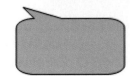

FIGURE 6.26 Item flipped vertically

1 Check that the layer containing the item to be flipped is the active layer in the **Layers** palette.

2 Click on the **Edit** menu.

3 Click on **Transform** (or **Transform Path**) (refer to Figure 6.17 on page 23).

4 From the submenu click on **Flip Horizontal** or **Flip Vertical**.

5 The direction of the image will change.

TIP!

To make a layer active, simply click on the layer name in the **Layers** palette.

Check your understanding *Flip an image*

1 In your artwork **quietsign**, select the layer **reading image**.

2 Flip the **reading** image **horizontally**.

3 Save the updated artwork keeping the filename **quietsign**.

Crop items

To crop an image is to cut out part of it. Cropping an image in Photoshop is done in a different way to cropping in other programs (e.g. Publisher or Word). In Photoshop, an area of the image is selected by drawing a frame (marquee) around it. The area within the frame is the part of the image that you want to keep (Figure 6.27).

An image **must** be cropped in a separate window. If you attempt to crop an image once it has been inserted into the artwork you will crop the entire artwork!

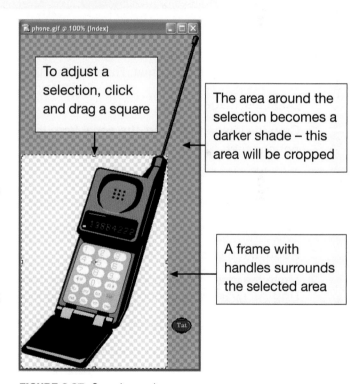

To adjust a selection, click and drag a square

The area around the selection becomes a darker shade – this area will be cropped

A frame with handles surrounds the selected area

FIGURE 6.27 Cropping an image

▶▶ *How to...*   crop an image

1 Follow steps 1–12 of 'How to... insert an image into artwork' on pages 24–25.

2 Fit the image on screen.

3 From the **Toolbox**, select the **Crop Tool** 🔲 .

4 Position the mouse at the top-left of the area to be retained within the image. Click and drag the mouse diagonally (from top-left to bottom-right) to draw a frame.

5 A frame with square handles displays around the selected area. The area outside the selection becomes a darker shade.

6 To amend the selected area, click and drag on a square handle.

7 Check the selection is correct.

8 Press the **Enter** key on the keyboard.

9 The area outside the selection will be cropped (cut out).

To copy and paste the image follow steps 13–26 of 'How to… insert an image into artwork' on page 25. A dialogue box will display asking if you want to save changes, click on **No**.

TIP!

If you have drawn an incorrect frame with the **Crop Tool** press the **Esc** key on the keyboard to deselect the frame.

TIP!

Once you have used the **Crop Tool** 🔲 select the **Move Tool** ⊹ to avoid making any accidental changes.

Check your understanding *Crop an image and insert it into the artwork*

For this task you will need the image file **phone** from the folder **files_imagecreation**. This image is provided in **gif** format. Refer to Layout Sketch 1 on page 20 or your printed copy.

1 Open the image **phone**.

2 Crop the image to remove the aerial from the top of the phone and the logo from the bottom right.

3 Copy the cropped image.

4 In your artwork **quietsign**, create a new layer named **phone image**

5 Paste the cropped image on to this layer.

6 **Reduce** the size of this image.

7 Move the image to be in the centre of the artwork, above the text USE OF MOBILE PHONES IS NOT PERMITTED

8 Close the original **phone** image without saving it.

9 Save the updated artwork keeping the filename **quietsign**.

▶▶ How to… *crop an image after it has been inserted on the artwork*

When you are updating the artwork, you may be required to crop an image that has already been placed into the artwork.

1   Select the layer containing the image to be cropped.

2   Create a new layer. This new layer should be positioned above the layer containing the image to be cropped.

3   Open the original image from your user area.

4   To crop the image, follow steps 2–8 in 'How to… crop an image' on page 29.

5   To paste the cropped image back into the artwork, follow steps 13–22 in 'How to… insert an image into artwork' on page 25.

6   Resize the image (refer to 'How to… resize an item (text, images, shapes) on a layer' on page 27). If there is no specific instruction about the image size, then resize it so that it is approximately the same size as before it was cropped.

7   Use the **Move Tool** to move the cropped image to the required position.

8   Delete the layer containing the image before it was cropped.

9   Save the updated artwork.

Creating graphic shapes

You will need to draw shapes using drawing tools and fill them with colour. Once you have learned how to create one shape you will find that all the others are created in a similar way.

After selecting the correct shape tool from the Toolbox you **must** check that the **Shape Layers** button ⬚ is selected in the **Options bar** before drawing the shape. The Paths button ⬚ must NOT be selected.

Shape Layers button

▶▶ How to...   *create a circle (fixed size)*

In Photoshop, circles and ovals are created using the **Ellipse Tool** and the related options in the **Options bar**. The **Ellipse Tool** may be hidden, as the tool displayed will be whichever shape tool was used last.

1   Insert a new layer using a suitable name.

2   Select the colour required for the shape by clicking in the **Set foreground color** square on the **Toolbox**.

3   In the **Toolbox**, right-click within the shape tool currently displayed. From the selection, click on the **Ellipse Tool** ⬭.

4   The **Ellipse Tool** will now display in the **Toolbox**.

5   In the **Options bar**, click the **Geometry options** drop-down arrow ▾ to the right of the shape tools.

6 The **Ellipse Options** window displays (Figure 6.28).

7 Click in the button for **Fixed Size** and enter the same figure for **W** (width) and **H** (height). Photoshop will insert **cm** (centimetres) after the numbers.

8 Check that the foreground colour you selected as the foreground colour is correctly displayed on the **Options bar**. If not, click in the colour square on the Options bar to open the **Color Picker** dialogue box.

9 Position the mouse in the artwork area. The mouse pointer will change to a cross.

10 Click once. The shape will be drawn.

11 Use the **Move Tool** to position the shape.

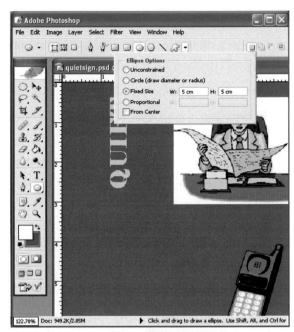

FIGURE 6.28 The **Ellipse Options** window

▶▶ How to... *create a freehand circle or an oval*

1 Follow steps 1–6 above.

2 In the **Ellipse Options** dialogue box:

To draw a circle: select the button for **Circle (draw diameter or radius)**.

To draw an oval: select the button for **Unconstrained**.

3 Position the mouse at the top-left of the area where the shape is to be drawn.

4 Click and drag the mouse diagonally from top-left to bottom-right to draw the shape.

> **TIP!**
> Once you have used a shape tool select the **Move Tool** ▸⊕ as a safety precaution.

> **TIP!**
> Zoom into the artwork when placing items:
> To **zoom in: Ctrl** and **+**
> To **zoom out: Ctrl** and **-**

Check your understanding *Create a circle*

Refer to **Layout Sketch 1** on page 20 or your printed copy.

1 In your artwork **quietsign** select the layer **reading image**. (*Note:* this is not the top layer because the circle needs to be behind the phone.)

2 Insert a new layer and call it **circle**

3 Set the foreground colour to **white**.

4 From the **Toolbox**, select the **Ellipse Tool**. Then, from the **Options bar**, select the option for a **Fixed Size** circle of **4 cm** wide and **4 cm** high.

5 Draw a circle in the centre of the artwork – the **phone** image should now be placed in the circle. Resize the phone image if required.

6 Use the **Move Tool** to position the circle and phone image correctly. Remember to select the correct layer in the **Layers** palette.

7 Save the updated artwork keeping the filename **quietsign**.

1   Insert a new layer using a suitable name.

2   Select the colour required by clicking in the **Set foreground color** square in the **Toolbox**.

3   From the **Toolbox**, right-click within the shape tool displayed.

4   From the selection of shape tools, click on the **Line Tool** \\.

5   In the **Options bar**, click in the **Weight** box and delete the contents (usually **1 px**).

6   Enter the required thickness for the line, followed by **px** (stands for pixels) Weight: 3 px . You must enter the **px** after the number otherwise Photoshop will enter **cm** and you will get a very thick line.

7   Check that the foreground colour you selected is correctly displayed on the **Options bar.** If not, click in the colour square on the Options bar to open the **Color Picker** dialogue box.

8   Move the mouse pointer into the artwork. The mouse pointer changes to a cross.

9   Position the mouse where you want to start drawing the line. Hold down the **Shift** key then click and drag the mouse to draw the line.

10 Release the mouse button and the Shift key.

11 Use the **Move Tool** to move the line if required.

TIP!

Hold down the **Shift** key when drawing lines to ensure the line is perfectly straight.

TIP!

Zoom into the artwork when placing items:

To **zoom in: Ctrl** and **+**
To **zoom out: Ctrl** and **-**

Check your understanding *Draw a line*

Refer to **Layout Sketch 1** on page 20 or your printed copy.

1 In your artwork **quietsign**, select the top layer **phone image**.

2 Insert a new layer and call it **line**

3 Set the foreground colour to **black**.

4 From the **Toolbox**, select the **Line Tool** then, on the **Options bar**, enter a line weight of **3 px** (remember to enter px).

5 Draw a diagonal line beginning below the bottom-left of the circle and ending above the top-right of the circle.

6 Use the **Move Tool** to position the line correctly.

7 Save the updated artwork keeping the filename **quietsign**.

1 Insert a new layer using a suitable name.

2 Set the foreground colour needed for the shape.

3 From the **Toolbox**, select the **Custom Shape Tool** 🎨. Remember, this may be hidden as the tool displayed in the **Toolbox** will be the last shape used.

4 On the **Options bar** click the **Geometry options** drop-down arrow ▼ to the right of the shape tools and select **Unconstrained** or **Fixed Size** as required.

5 Check that the foreground colour selected is correctly displayed on the **Options bar**. If not, click in the colour square on the Options bar to open the **Color Picker** dialogue box.

6 On the **Options bar**, click on the drop-down arrow to the right of **Shape** (Figure 6.29).

7 The **Custom Shape Picker** window displays.

8 Scroll down to see other shapes.

9 Click to select a shape. Move the mouse into the artwork and draw the shape.

If the shape is not displayed:

a. Click ▶ to display more options (Figure 6.29).

b. A menu displays. Select the category of shapes or click **All**.

c. A dialogue box displays. Click **Append**.

d. More shapes will now be displayed in the **Custom Shape Picker** window. Scroll down to see all the available shapes.

e. Select and draw the shape.

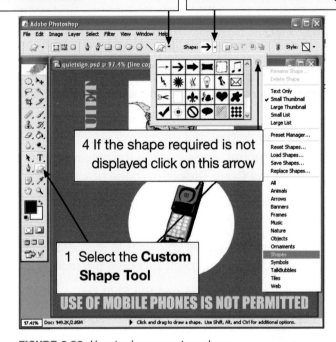

2 Click on the drop-down arrow and select **Unconstrained** or **Fixed Size**

3 Click on the drop-down arrow to view the available shapes (remember to scroll down to see all the shapes)

4 If the shape required is not displayed click on this arrow

1 Select the **Custom Shape Tool**

FIGURE 6.29 How to draw a custom shape

TIP!

Once you have used a shape tool, select the **Move Tool** as a safety precaution.

TIP!

To draw a shape, drag the mouse diagonally from top-left to bottom-right.

Refer to **Layout Sketch 1** on page 20 or your printed copy.

1 In your artwork **quietsign**, create a new layer and call it **arrow**

2 Set the foreground colour to a **dark green**.

3 Select the **Custom Shape Tool**. From the **Options bar**, in the **Custom Shape Picker** window, select an arrow shape.

4 Draw an arrow below the word **QUIET** to the left of the circle (the arrow will point to the right at this stage).

5 Rotate the layer arrow **90° anticlockwise** (CCW).

6 Move the arrow to the position shown in the layout sketch.

7 Save the artwork keeping the filename **quietsign**.

Printing artwork and images

For OCR assignments it is critical that the artwork that you create and update are printed in colour. Black-and-white printouts of the artwork are not acceptable. The images may need to be printed in colour or black-and-white as instructed.

▶▶ How to... *print artwork or images in colour*

Check that you are connected to a colour printer and that you are sending the artwork to the colour printer.

1 Click on the **File** menu.

2 Click on **Print with Preview**.

3 The **Print** dialogue box displays (Figure 6.30).

4 Check that the **Scaled Print Size** is **100%** (this is the actual size of the artwork).

5 In Photoshop, the preview on the left will be in colour, even if you are connected to a black-and-white printer.

6 Do not be concerned that the artwork height and width are marginally different by a few millimetres to the size you originally entered, Photoshop adjusts the size. This is acceptable.

7 Click **Print**.

8 A second **Print** dialogue box displays (Figure 6.31).

9 Check that the number of copies is set to **1**.

FIGURE 6.30 Previewing a printout

FIGURE 6.31 The **Print** dialogue box

10 Click on **OK**.

11 The artwork will be printed. Check the printout carefully to ensure that all colours are displayed correctly.

Check your understanding *Print the artwork in colour and close*

1 Print one copy of your artwork **quietsign** in colour.

2 Close the artwork. Write your name and centre number on the printout.

▶▶ How to... *draw a rectangle*

1 Insert a new layer and select a foreground colour.

2 From the **Toolbox**, select the **Rectangle Tool** ▫, or the **Rounded Rectangle Tool** ▢.

3 On the **Options bar**, click the **Geometry options** drop-down arrow ▾ to the right-hand side of the shape tools, select **Fixed Size** and enter a fixed size or, to draw a freehand rectangle, click in the button for **Unconstrained**.

4 Move the mouse into the artwork and draw the shape.

> **TIP!**
>
> Once you have used a shape tool, select the **Move Tool** ▸₊ as a safety precaution.

▶▶ How to... *draw a triangle*

1 Insert a new layer and select a foreground colour.

2 From the **Toolbox**, select the **Polygon Tool** ⬡.

3 On the **Options bar**, click in the box for **Sides** `Sides: 3` and enter the number **3**.

4 Move the mouse into the artwork and draw the shape.

▶▶ How to... *draw a star or starburst shape*

1 Insert a new layer and select a foreground colour.

2 From the **Toolbox**, select the **Polygon Tool** ⬡.

3 On the **Options bar**, click the **Geometry options** ▾ drop-down arrow to the right of the shape tools.

4 A **Polygon Options** window displays. Click in the box for **Star** (Figure 6.32).

5 Click in the box for **Sides** and enter the number of sides required.

6 To draw a starburst shape, enter approximately 9–12 sides or use the **Custom Shape Tool**.

7 Move the mouse into the artwork and draw the shape.

FIGURE 6.32
Drawing a star shape

1   Create a new piece of artwork as follows:

Name:	**shapes**
Width:	**15 cm**
Height	**10 cm**
Resolution:	**78 pixels/cm**
Mode:	**RGB color**
Contents:	**White**

TIP!

Remember to create and name a new layer for each shape and set the foreground colour before you draw each shape.

2   Draw a **blue** rectangle **3 cm** wide and **2 cm** high in the top-left of the artwork.

3   Draw a **yellow** square **3 cm wide** and **3 cm high** in the top-right of the artwork.

4   Draw a **brown 8-sided** star in the centre of the artwork.

5   Use the **outline heart** from the custom shapes to draw a **blue** heart-shaped outline in the bottom-right of the artwork. The entire heart shape should not have a solid fill. The white background colour should be visible through the centre of the heart.

6   Draw a **black 3-sided** triangle in the bottom-left of the artwork.

7   Draw a **red 5-sided** polygon in the bottom-centre of the artwork.

8   Save the artwork using the filename **shapes**

9   Print one copy in colour. Write your name on the printout.

10 Close the artwork and exit Photoshop.

TIP!

To change the colour of a shape after it has been drawn, or for a copied shape, double-click in the colour displayed (the layer thumbnail) for that shape layer in the **Layers** palette to open the **Color Picker** dialogue box.

ASSESS YOUR SKILLS – Insert images, create shapes and manipulate items (text, images, shapes)

By working through Section 2 you will have learnt the skills listed below. Read each item to help you decide how confident you feel about each skill.

- open existing artwork
- rotate an item
- insert an image into artwork
  - open the image
  - copy an image
  - paste the copied image into the artwork
  - close the original image
- resize an original image and an item on a layer
- flip an item
- crop an image
- create a circle (fixed size and freehand)
- draw a line
- draw custom shapes
- print in colour
- draw a rectangle, a triangle, a star and a starburst.

If you think you need more practice on any of the skills above, go back and work through the skill(s) again.

If you feel confident, move on to Section 3.

Section 3: Amend artwork, set resolution and work with digital images

LEARNING OUTCOMES

In this section you will learn how to:

- save artwork using a different filename
- copy an item and move the copy
- change the colour of a copied shape
- amend and resize text
- change the resolution of a provided image
- take a screen print of the amended resolution
- save an image in jpg format and gif format
- open a digital picture, reduce the picture size and enter text
- convert an image to greyscale.

Note: The accompanying CD-ROM includes two handouts – 'Using ruler guides to align items' and 'How to... download digital pictures from a camera'.

▶▶ How to... save artwork using a different filename

1 Click on the **File** menu.

2 Click on **Save as**.

3 The **Save as** dialogue box displays.

4 In the **File name** box delete the existing filename.

5 Enter the new filename. Click on **Save**.

6 A **Photoshop Format Options** dialogue box may display. Click on **OK**.

Deleting items (text, images, shapes)

When you need to delete an item in Photoshop you should delete the entire layer containing that item. Refer to 'How to... delete a layer' on page 17.

Check your understanding *Delete an item*

1 Open your artwork **quietsign** and save it using the new filename **notice**

2 Select the layer named **circle** and delete this layer.

3 Save the artwork keeping the filename **notice**.

Copying items

You will need to copy an image or shape. Another term for copy is **duplicate**. In Photoshop the easiest way to copy an image or shape is to **duplicate the layer** that contains the original item.

▶▶ How to... *copy an item and move the copy*

1. In the **Layers** palette select the layer containing the item to be copied.

2. Click on the **Layer** menu.

3. Click on **Duplicate Layer**.

4. The **Duplicate Layer** dialogue box will open.

5. Photoshop will suggest the original layer name followed by the word **copy** (Figure 6.33).

6. Click on **OK**.

FIGURE 6.33 Copying a layer

7. The copied item may not be visible on the artwork because it is positioned in the same position as the original.

8. The copied layer will be displayed in the **Layers** palette (Figure 6.34).

9. If you copy a layer containing a shape, notice that a link symbol displays on the original layer and the copied layer.

10. To move the copied item, select the copied layer in the **Layers** palette.

11. From the **Toolbox**, select the **Move Tool** and click and drag the copied item to the required position.

> **TIP!**
>
> If the link symbol is not displayed on the copied layer you will not be able to make any changes to the copy. Simply click in the Layers palette where the link should be to display the link again.

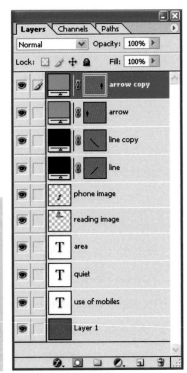

FIGURE 6.34 The **Layers** palette showing copied layers

▶▶ How to... *change the colour of a copied shape*

1. Select the copied shape.

2. Double-click in the colour square displayed for that shape layer in the **Layers** palette.

3. The **Color Picker** dialogue box will open.

4. Select a colour.

5. Click on **OK**.

6. The colour of the copied shape will change.

Refer to Layout Sketch 2 or your printed copy.

1 In your artwork **notice**, select the layer containing the **arrow**.

2 **Copy** this layer. Keep the layer name suggested by Photoshop: **arrow copy**

3 Move the copied arrow to the right of the artwork as shown in **Layout Sketch 2** (Figure 6.35).

4 Select the layer with the **line**.

5 Copy the line. Keep the name suggested by Photoshop: **line copy**

6 **Flip** the copied line **horizontally**.

7 Save the artwork keeping the filename **notice**

Refer to the handout on the CD-ROM titled 'Using ruler guides to align items'.

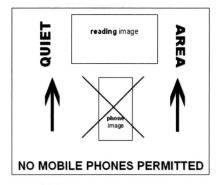

FIGURE 6.35 Layout Sketch 2

Amending text

You will need to amend some existing text and its formatting (e.g. resize it) on the artwork. You can also use these guidelines to amend the text or text formatting on the original artwork.

▶▶ How to... *amend text*

1 In your artwork, select the layer containing the text to be amended.

2 Select the **Horizontal Type Tool** T .

3 Click within the text. A cursor will display within the text frame.

4 Delete the unwanted text. Use the **Delete** key to delete text to the right of the cursor or the **Backspace** key to delete text to the left of the cursor.

5 Use the **Move Tool** ▶⊕ to move the text if required.

> **TIP!**
>
> To move text use the **Move Tool** or hold down the **Ctrl** key and tap the **arrow** key.

▶▶ How to... *resize text*

1 In your artwork select the layer containing the text to be amended.

2 Select the **Horizontal Type Tool** T .

3 Click within the text. The text frame will display with a flashing cursor.

4 Click and drag to highlight the text (begin at either end of the text).

5 In the **Options bar** click on the drop-down arrow to the right of the **Set the font size** box. A list of sizes displays. Click to select a font size. Alternatively, click in the font size box and enter a size 22 pt.

6 Click on a square handle to extend/reduce the text frame as required.

7 Click on the **Move Tool** from the **Toolbox** to deselect the text frame and move the text if required.

Check your understanding *Amend text*

1 In your artwork **notice**, select the text layer named **use of mobiles**.

2 Amend the text to **NO MOBILE PHONES PERMITTED**

3 Resize the text so that it fills the width of the artwork. The text must remain within the artwork and must not touch any edges.

4 Save the artwork keeping the filename **notice**

5 Print one copy in colour. Write your name and centre number on the printout.

6 Close the artwork.

Changing the resolution of a provided image

For an explanation of resolution, refer to 'Understanding resolution' on page 10.

You will be provided with an image for which you will need to change the resolution. If the pixel dimensions are reduced, this will result in the image becoming more **pixilated** (the individual squares that make up an image will become more noticeable). If there is text on the image this will usually become 'fuzzier'. You will not always be instructed to maintain the original image size, however this is expected.

▶▶ How to... *change the resolution of an image*

1 Open the image from within Photoshop (refer to 'How to... open an image' on page 22).

2 Click on the **Image** menu.

3 Click on **Image Size**.

4 The **Image Size** dialogue box displays.

5 Make sure there is a tick in the box for **Constrain Proportions** (Figure 6.36).

6 In the **Document Size** section click on the drop-down arrow to the right of the **Resolution** box and select **pixels/cm**.

7 Click in the **Resolution** box and enter the new resolution.

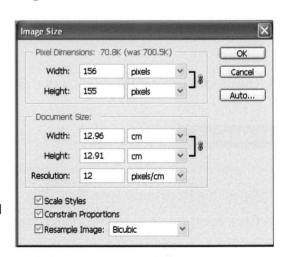

FIGURE 6.36 Amending the resolution

8   Refer to 'How to... take a screen print of the amended resolution' below.

9   In the **Image Size** dialogue box, click on **OK**.

10 The resolution will change and the size of the image on screen will also change. The actual image size will not change.

11 Fit the image on screen (**View** menu, **Fit on Screen**).

12 Notice the change in the quality of the image.

The examples below show an image where the resolution has been reduced.

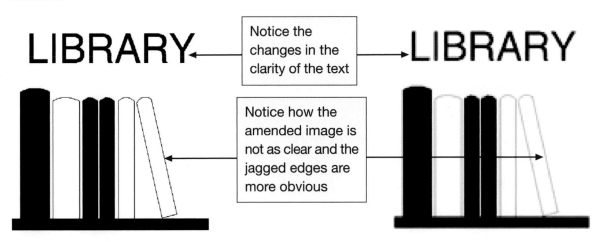

FIGURE 6.37 The original image

FIGURE 6.38 The effect of reducing the resolution

▶▶ How to... *take a screen print of the amended resolution*

Make sure the **Image Size** dialogue box is open and that you have entered the new resolution.

To take the screen print:

1   Press the **Print Screen** key on the keyboard.

2   You have taken a picture of the screen but you will not see any change on-screen.

To start Microsoft Word:

3   Click on the **Start** button.

4   Click on **All Programs**.

5   Click on **Microsoft Office**.

6   Click on **Microsoft Office Word 2003**.

7   A new blank document will open.

To paste the screen print into the open Word document:

8   Click on the **Edit** menu then click on **Paste**.

9   You may enter your name anywhere in the screen print document or handwrite it later.

To save the screen print:

10   In **Microsoft Word**, click on the **File** menu.

11   Click on **Save As**.

12   The **Save As** dialogue box displays.

13   Click on the drop-down arrow to the right of **Save in** then double-click to open the required folder(s) in your user area.

14   In the **File name** box, delete any text (e.g. Doc1).

15   Enter the required filename.

16   Click on **Save**.

To print the screen print:

17   Click the **Print** icon 🖨 on the **toolbar**.

To close the screen print document and exit Word:

18   Click on the **File** menu.

19   Click on **Close**.

20   Click on the **File** menu again.

21   Click on **Exit**.

Saving in different file formats

▶▶ How to...   *save an image in jpg format*

1   Click on the **File** menu.

2   Click on **Save as**.

3   The **Save As** dialogue box displays.

4   Click on the drop-down arrow to the right of **Save in**. Double-click to open the folder in your user area where the file is to be saved.

5   In the **File name** box, enter the required filename.

6   Click on the drop-down arrow to the right of **Format**.

7   A list of file types displays (Figure 6.39).

8   Click on **JPEG (*.JPG,*.JPEG,*.JPE)**.

9   Click on **Save**.

10   A **JPEG Options** dialogue box displays (Figure 6.40).

11   Click on **OK**.

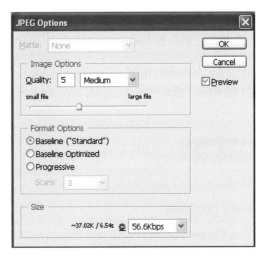

FIGURE 6.39 The **Save As** dialogue box

FIGURE 6.40 The **JPEG Options** dialogue box

▶▶ How to... *save an image in gif format*

1 Follow steps 1–7 of 'How to… save an image in jpg format' on page 44.

2 From the list of available formats click on **CompuServe GIF (*.GIF)**.

3 An **Indexed Color** dialogue box displays.

4 Click on **OK**.

5 A **GIF Options** dialogue box then displays.

6 Click on **OK**.

Check your understanding
Amend the resolution and take a screen print

1 Open the image **library**.

2 Change the resolution of this image to **12 pixels/cm**. Make sure you maintain the original image proportions.

3 Take a screen print of the dialogue box showing the changed resolution.

4 You may enter your name on the page containing the screen print or handwrite it after you have printed it.

5 Save and print the screen print.

6 Save the changed image as a **jpg** file using the filename **books**

7 Print the image **books**.

8 Write your name and the date on the printout of the **books** image.

Downloading digital pictures

There are many different makes of digital camera available and the installation and use of each may vary. You should follow the installation and usage instructions in the user manual for your camera.

If the digital pictures are going to be provided for you by your tutor, refer to 'How to... open a digital picture in Photoshop' below. If you have access to a digital camera and the opportunity to take and/or download the pictures yourself, refer to the handout on the accompanying CD-ROM titled 'How to... download digital pictures'.

▶▶ *How to...* open a digital picture in Photoshop

1 Click on the **File** menu.

2 Click on **Open**.

3 The **Open** dialogue box will display.

4 Click on the drop-down arrow to the right of the **Look in** box and open the folder containing the downloaded images.

5 In the **Files of type** box make sure that **All Formats** is selected.

6 In the main window click on the name of the image.

7 The image will be highlighted (usually blue) and a miniature of the image will display at the bottom of the **Open** dialogue box.

8 Click **Open**.

9 The picture may be quite large. Check the print size (**View** menu, **Print Size**) and reduce the size if necessary. Click on **File**, **Print with Preview** to make sure that the image will fit on an A4 sheet of paper when printed.

10 Rotate the image if required (**Image** menu, **Rotate Canvas**, **90° CW** or **90° CCW**).

> **TIP!**
>
> Check the size of the digital image and amend this if required before you enter any text on the image.

▶▶ *How to...* reduce the size of a digital picture

1 Click on the **Image** menu.

2 Click on **Image Size**.

3 The **Image Size** dialogue box displays.

4 Check that there is a tick in the box for **Constrain Proportions**.

5 In the **Document Size** section, click in the **Width** box and enter a size. The **Height** will be adjusted by Photoshop and the image proportion will be maintained.

6 Click on **OK**.

1 In the **Toolbox**, click in the **Set foreground color** square and select a colour that will show clearly on your picture.

2 From the **Toolbox** select the **Horizontal Type Tool**.

3 From the **Options bar** select a suitable font and font size.

4 Draw a text frame anywhere on the picture.

5 Enter the required text.

6 Use the **Move Tool** to deselect the text frame and move the text if required. Make sure the text can be clearly seen.

8 Save the updated digital picture into your user area, using a suitable filename in a suitable file format, usually **jpg** format. (Refer to 'How to… save an image in jpg format' on page 44.)

Printing in black and white

You may need to print the image with the amended resolution and/or the image taken using a digital camera in either black and white or colour. To review the method for printing in colour refer to 'How to… print artwork or images in colour' on page 35.

A quick way to print in black and white is simply to print the image on a black-and-white printer. Alternatively, your tutor may convert the image for you, or you may convert the image to greyscale yourself.

▶▶ **How to...** *convert an image to greyscale*

1 Open the image in Photoshop.

2 Click on the **Image** menu.

3 Click on **Mode**.

4 Click on **Grayscale**.

5 A dialogue box displays (Figure 6.41).

6 Click on **OK**.

7 The image will convert to shades of **black and white**.

FIGURE 6.41 Converting an image to greyscale

For this task you may use the image **study1**, **study2** or **study3** from the folder **files_imgcreation**, or take a picture of a **library** or **study area** using a digital camera, or you may use a picture of a **library** or **study area** taken using a digital camera provided by a tutor.

1   Open the picture of a **library** or **study area** taken using a digital camera.

2   Check the size of the image. It should not be wider than **20 cm** or taller than **28 cm.** If required, reduce the size of the image.

3   Rotate the image if necessary.

4   From the **Toolbox**, select a foreground colour that will display clearly on the picture.

5   Select the **Horizontal Type Tool** and enter your name anywhere on the picture.

6   Convert the image to greyscale.

7   Save the picture in **jpg** format using the filename **workarea**

8   Print the image **workarea**.

9   Close the image.

10 Exit Photoshop.

ASSESS YOUR SKILLS – Amend artwork, set resolution and work with digital pictures

By working through Section 3 you will have learnt the skills listed below. Read each item to help you decide how confident you feel about each skill.

- ⊙ save artwork using a different filename
- ⊙ copy an item and move the copy
- ⊙ change the colour of a copied shape
- ⊙ amend and resize text
- ⊙ change the resolution of a provided image
- ⊙ take a screen print of the amended resolution
- ⊙ save an image in jpg format and gif format
- ⊙ open a digital picture, reduce the picture size and enter text
- ⊙ convert an image to greyscale.

If you think you need more practice on any of the skills above, go back and work through the skill(s) again.

If you feel confident, do the Build-up and Practice tasks on pages 55–64.

Click means click with the left mouse button

Keep a copy of this page next to you. Refer to it when working through tasks and during any assessments.

QUICK REFERENCE – Create artwork using layers

HOW TO	METHOD
Start Photoshop	Click the **Start** button → select **All Programs** → **Adobe Photoshop CS**.
Select a hidden tool from the Toolbox	Right-click anywhere within a tool in the **Toolbox** → the hidden tools will display → click to select a tool.
Close palettes	Click the red cross at the top right corner of the palette window.
Display palettes	Click the **Window** menu → click on the name of the palette required, e.g. Layers.
Create a new piece of artwork	Click the **File** menu → click on **New** → the **New** dialogue box displays → enter the name in the **Name** box → click the drop-down arrow next to the **Width** and **Height** boxes and select **cm** → enter the width in the **Width** box → enter the height in the **Height** box → click the drop-down arrow next to the **Resolution** box and select **pixels/cm** → enter the resolution in the **Resolution** box → click the drop-down arrow next to the **Color Mode** box and select **RGB Color** → click the drop-down arrow to the right of **Background Contents** and select **Transparent** → click **OK**.
Set the orientation	Click the **File** menu → click on **Page Setup** → in the **Page Setup** dialogue box click on the button for **Portrait** or **Landscape** → click **OK**.
Change the view on screen	Before printing and to see the actual size: Click on the **View** menu → click **Print Size**. Whilst working on the artwork click on the **View** menu → click **Fit on Screen**.
Zoom in	Hold down the **Ctrl** key and tap the **+** key.
Zoom out	Hold down the **Ctrl** key and tap the **–** key.
Save artwork as a Photoshop file	Click the **File** menu → click on **Save As** → the **Save As** dialogue box displays → click the drop-down arrow to the right of **Save in** → click on your user area → in the **File name** box enter the filename → in the **Format** box make sure that **Photoshop (*.PSD,*.PDD)** is selected → check that the **Layers** box is ticked → click **Save**.
Select a foreground colour	From the **Toolbox** click in the **Set foreground color** square → the **Color Picker** dialogue box displays → click in the large square to select a colour or, to view other colours, click in the vertical bar, then click in the large colour square to select a colour → click **OK**.
Fill the background with a colour	Remember the **Paint Bucket Tool** will fill with the colour in the **Set foreground color** box! Set the foreground color to the colour needed to fill the artwork background → select the **Paint Bucket Tool** → on the **Options bar** click the drop-down arrow to the right of the **Fill** box → select **Foreground** → move the mouse on to the artwork → click once.

HOW TO	METHOD
Save an updated file	Click the File menu → click on Save.
Insert a new layer	Click on the Layer menu → click on New → click on Layer → the New Layer dialogue box displays → in the Name box enter a suitable name → click OK.
Make a layer active	Click on the layer name in the Layers palette.
Insert text	Select the foreground color → from the Toolbox select the Horizontal Type Tool → in the Options bar click the drop-down arrow to the right of the Set the font family box → a list of fonts displays → click to select a font → click the drop-down arrow to the right of the Set the font size box → a list of sizes displays → click to select a font size → click and drag the mouse to draw a text frame → enter the required text → select the Move Tool to deselect the text frame.
Highlight text	Select the required text layer → select the Horizontal Type Tool → click and drag the mouse from one end of the text to the other.
Format text	Select the Horizontal Type Tool → highlight the text → select the options required on the Options bar → click on the Move Tool to deselect the text frame.
Move an item (text, shape or an image)	Select the correct layer → select the Move Tool → click and drag to move the item.
Close artwork or image	Click the File menu → click on Close.
Exit Photoshop	Click the File menu → click on Exit.

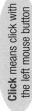

Click means click with the left mouse button

Keep a copy of this page next to you. Refer to it when working through tasks and during any assessments.

QUICK REFERENCE – *Insert images, create shapes and manipulate items*

HOW TO	METHOD
Rotate an item (text, image, shape)	Select the layer containing the item to be rotated → click the **Edit** menu → **Transform** (or **Transform Path** if the layer contains a shape) → select **Rotate 180°** or **Rotate 90° CW** or **Rotate 90° CCW**.
Insert an image into artwork	Create a **new layer** using a suitable name → open the image (see 'How to open an image or artwork') → select the image by clicking on its **title bar** → click the **Select** menu → click on **All** → click the **Edit** menu → click on **Copy** → click on the **title bar** of the artwork to select it → select the correct layer → click the **Edit** menu → click on **Paste** → use the **Move Tool** to move the image if required → select the image by clicking on its **title bar**. If it is not visible click on the **Window** menu and select the image from the list → click the **File** menu → click **Close**.
Open an image or artwork	Click on the **File** menu → click on **Open** → the **Open** dialogue box displays → click the drop-down arrow to the right of **Look in** and locate the image → click on the image → click **Open**.
Resize an item (text, images, shape) on a layer	Select the layer → click the **Edit** menu → click on **Transform** (or **Transform Path**) → click on **Scale** → handles surround the image → on the **Options** bar click on the **Maintain aspect ratio** symbol → click and drag a corner handle or, on the **Options** bar, enter a number in the **W** (Width) box → select the **Move Tool** → a dialogue box displays → click **Apply**.
Flip an item (image or shape)	Select the layer → click on the **Edit** menu → click on **Transform** (or **Transform Path**) → click **Flip Horizontal** or **Flip Vertical**.
Crop an image	Select the **Crop Tool** → click and drag the mouse diagonally to draw a frame around the part of the image to be kept → press the **Enter** key on the keyboard. If it is to be cropped on the amended artwork, open the original image, crop it and insert it as a new layer → delete the entire layer containing the original image.
Print the artwork or image	Click the **File** menu → click on **Print with Preview** → the **Print** dialogue box displays → check that the scaled print size is 100% → click **Print** → a second **Print** dialogue box displays → click **OK**.
Create a circle (fixed size)	Insert a new layer with a suitable name → set the foreground colour → select the **Ellipse Tool** → on the **Options** bar click the **Geometry options** drop-down arrow → the **Ellipse Options** window displays → click on the button for **Fixed Size** → enter the same figure for **W** (width) and **H** (height) → position the mouse in the artwork area → click once.

HOW TO	METHOD
Create a circle (freehand) or an oval	Insert a new layer with a suitable name → set the foreground colour → select the **Ellipse Tool** → on the **Options bar** click the **Geometry** options drop-down arrow → the **Ellipse Options** window displays → click on the button for **Circle (draw diameter or radius)** → position the mouse in the artwork area → click and drag the mouse to draw a circle or an oval.
Draw a line	Insert a new layer with a suitable name → set the foreground colour → select the **Line Tool** → on the **Options bar** click in the **Weight** box → delete the contents → enter a suitable line thickness followed by px → move the mouse into the artwork → hold down the **Shift key** → click and drag the mouse to draw the line.
Draw custom shapes	Insert a new layer with a suitable name → set the foreground colour → select the **Custom Shape Tool** → on the **Options bar** click the **Geometry** options drop-down arrow → select **Unconstrained** or **Fixed Size** as required → on the **Options bar** click the drop-down arrow to the right of **Shape** → the **Custom Shape Picker** window displays → select a shape. If the shape is not displayed click the more options arrow → a menu displays → select the category of shapes or click **All** → a dialogue box displays → click **Append** → select a shape → move the mouse into the artwork → click and drag the mouse to draw the shape (or click once if you have selected **Fixed Size**).
Draw a rectangle	Insert a new layer with a suitable name → set the foreground colour → select the **Rectangle Tool** → on the **Options bar** click the **Geometry** options drop-down arrow to the right of the shape tools and either enter a fixed size or, to draw a freehand rectangle, click in the button for **Unconstrained** → move the mouse into the artwork and draw the shape (or click once if you have selected **Fixed Size**).
Draw a triangle	Insert a new layer with a suitable name → set the foreground colour → select the **Polygon Tool** → on the **Options bar** click in the box for **Sides** and enter the number 3 → click and drag the mouse to draw the triangle.
Draw a star or starburst	Insert a new layer with a suitable name → set the foreground colour → select the **Polygon Tool** → on the **Options bar** click the **Geometry** options drop-down arrow → a **Polygon Options** window displays → click in the box for **Star** → enter the number of sides in the **Sides** box → move the mouse on to the artwork → click and drag the mouse to draw the shape. A starburst shape can also be found in the custom shapes.

QUICK REFERENCE – Amend artwork, set resolution and work with digital pictures

Keep a copy of this page next to you.
Refer to it when working through
tasks and during any assessments.

HOW TO	METHOD
Delete an item (image, text, shape)	Select the layer containing the item to be deleted → click on the **Layer** menu → click on **Delete** → click on **Layer** → a dialogue box displays → click **Yes**.
Copy an item	Select the layer containing the item to be copied → click on the **Layer** menu → click on **Duplicate Layer** → the **Duplicate Layer** dialogue box displays → Photoshop suggests the original layer name followed by copy → click **OK**.
Move a copied item	Select the copied layer → select the **Move Tool** → click and drag the copied item to the required position.
Display rulers	Click the **View** menu → if there is no tick before Rulers → click on **Rulers**.
Display a ruler guide on the artwork	Position the mouse pointer in the white ruler area → the pointer changes to a white arrow → click and drag the mouse button from the white ruler area to the artwork.
Move a ruler guide	Position the mouse pointer on the ruler guide → click and drag the guide to the required position.
Remove a ruler guide	Position the mouse pointer on the ruler guide → click and drag the guide off the artwork.
Amend text	Select the layer containing the text to be amended → select the **Horizontal Type Tool** → click within the text → a cursor will display → delete the unwanted text → enter the new text.
Reformat text	Select the layer containing the text to be amended → select the **Horizontal Type Tool** → click within the text → a text frame displays → click and drag the text frame to adjust it if required → highlight the text → on the **Options bar** click the drop-down arrow to the right of the **Set the font size box** and select a font size or enter a size → select the **Move Tool** to deselect the text frame.
Change the resolution of an image	Open the image from within Photoshop → click on the **Image** menu → **Image Size** → the **Image Size** dialogue box displays → check there is a tick for **Constrain Proportions** → in the **Document Size** section click the drop-down arrow to the right of the **Resolution** box and select pixels/cm → enter the new resolution in the **Resolution** box → take a screen print, then click **OK**.

HOW TO	METHOD
Take a screen print of the amended resolution	Make sure the **Image Size** dialogue box is open and that you have entered the new resolution → press the **Print Screen** key on the keyboard → click the **Start** button → click **All Programs** → **Microsoft Office** → **Microsoft Office Word** → a new blank document will open → click on the **Paste** icon → enter your name anywhere in the document (or handwrite it later) → click on the **File** menu → **Save As** → the **Save As** window displays → click the drop-down arrow to the right of **Save in** then double-click to open your working folder → delete any text in the **File name** box → enter the filename → click on **Save** → click the **Print** icon → click on the **File** menu → **Close** → click on the **File** menu again → click **Exit**.
Convert an image to greyscale	Open the image in Photoshop → click the **Image** menu → click on **Mode** → click on **Grayscale** → a dialogue box displays asking if you want to **Discard color information** → click **OK**.
Save an image in jpg format	Click the **File** menu → click on **Save As** → the **Save As** dialogue box displays → click the drop-down arrow next to **Save in** and open the folder where the file is to be saved → in the **File name** box enter the filename → click the drop-down to the right of **Format** → a list of file types displays → click on **JPEG (*.JPG,*.JPEG,*.JPE)** → click on **Save** → a **JPEG Options** dialogue box displays → click **OK**.
Save an image in gif format	Click the **File** menu → click on **Save As** → the **Save As** dialogue box displays → click the drop-down arrow next to **Save in** and open the folder where the file is to be saved → in the **File name** box enter the filename → click the drop-down arrow to the right of **Format** → a list of file types displays → click on **CompuServe GIF (*.GIF)** → an **Indexed Color** dialogue box displays → click **OK** → a **GIF Options** dialogue box displays → click **OK**.
Download digital pictures from a camera	Open the **My Computer** window → connect the lead from the digital camera to the USB port on the computer → a **Found New Hardware** dialogue box may display on the task bar (you may need to press a button on your camera/docking bay) → in the **My Computer** window a digital camera icon should display → double-click the camera icon → a digital camera window opens → click on **Get pictures from camera** → a **Scanner and Camera Wizard** dialogue box will display, click **Next** → select the pictures to download → click **Next** → enter the name and location (folder) for the pictures, click **Next** → a dialogue box will display. The button for **Nothing. I'm finished with these pictures** will be selected, click **Next** → a dialogue box will display → click **Finish**.
Open a digital picture in Photoshop	Click the **File** menu → click on **Open** → the **Open** dialogue box will display → click the drop-down arrow to the right of the **Look in** box and open the folder containing the images → click on the name of the image → click **Open**. Check the print size: **View** menu → **Print Size**. Preview the printout: **File** menu → **Print with Preview**. Rotate the image if required: **Image** menu → **Rotate Canvas** → **90° CW** or **CCW**.
Reduce the size of a digital picture	Click the **Image** menu → click on **Image Size** → the **Image Size** dialogue box displays → check that there is a tick for **Constrain Proportions** → under **Document Size** click in the **Width** box and enter the new width → click **OK**.
Enter text on a digital picture	Select a suitable foreground colour → select the **Horizontal Type Tool** → from the Options bar select a suitable font and font size → draw a text frame on the picture → enter the text → use the **Move Tool** to deselect the text frame and move the text if required.

Build-up tasks

Candidate instructions for the artwork

All images:

- must not be distorted
- may be resized to suit the artwork
- must not touch or overlap any other items or the edge of the artwork.

All text:

- must not touch or overlap any other items or the edge of the artwork.

(Note that all items will be placed on the background layer)

Filename: card

resized **stars** image		flipped copy of **stars** image

A GIFT

FOR YOU

cropped **border** image

Thinking of you on this special day

Build-up Task Layout Sketch 1

Filename: gift

stars image	

A GIFT

FOR YOU

border image

Thinking of you today and always

Build-up Task Layout Sketch 2

You will need the file **stars** from the folder **files_imgcreation**.

Refer to **Build-up Task Layout Sketch 1** and the 'Candidate instructions for the artwork' on page 55.

1 **a)** Create a new piece of artwork which is **8 cm** wide by **10 cm** tall.
   b) Fill the background with **yellow**.

2 Draw a **black** straight line running the entire height of the artwork and position it on the right of the artwork as shown in **Layout Sketch 1**.

3 **a)** Enter the following text in **red**:

   Thinking of you on this special day

   b) Rotate this text **90° anticlockwise (CCW)** and position it on the right of the artwork as shown in **Layout Sketch 1**.
   c) Size this text to fill most of the height of the artwork.

4 **a)** Import the image **stars** and position it at the top left of the artwork.
   b) Resize this image so that it is visibly smaller than the original image.

5 **a)** Copy the image **stars**.
   b) Flip this copy **vertically** and position the copy in the top right of the artwork.
   c) The flipped image should be the same size as the original image.

6 Save your artwork using the filename **card**

> **TIP!**
>
> In an OCR assignment the resolution will not be specified. Select a resolution between 60 to 78 pixels/cm.

> **TIP!**
>
> The line thickness may not be specified, refer to the Layout Sketch and select an appropriate line weight.

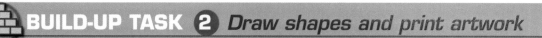

You will need the file **border** from the folder **files_imgcreation**.

Refer to **Build-up Task Layout Sketch 1** and the 'Candidate instructions for the artwork' on page 55.

Continue working on your artwork named **card** that you saved in Build-up Task 1.

1 **a)** Open the image **border**.
   b) Crop the image to remove **all** of the green border from the right side of the image.
   c) Insert the image on the artwork.
   d) Rotate the image **90° anticlockwise (CCW)**.

   You may resize the image to fit as shown on **Build-up Task Layout Sketch 1**.

2 **a)** Create a red **heart** shape with a thick outline in the centre of your artwork.
   b) Make sure the heart shape does not have a solid fill – the yellow background of the artwork must be visible through the middle of the heart shape.

3 Enter the following text in **dark green** above the heart shape:

   A GIFT

4 **a)** Enter the following text in **dark green** below the heart shape:

   FOR YOU

   b) Use the same font and text size as you did for the text A GIFT

5 Save your artwork keeping the filename **card**

6 Check your artwork to make sure that you have placed all items according to **Build-up Task Layout Sketch 1** and that you have carried out the 'Candidate instructions for the artwork'.

7 Print one copy of your artwork in colour.

8 On the printout write **your name**, **your centre number** and **the date** anywhere below the artwork.

Refer to **Build-up Task Layout Sketch 2** and the 'Candidate instructions for the artwork' on page 55.

Continue working on your artwork called **card** that you saved in Build-up Task 2.

1 Open your saved artwork **card** (if it is not already open) and save it using the new filename **gift** (in Photoshop file format .psd).

2 Delete the copied image **stars** from the top right of the artwork.

3 a) Amend the text **Thinking of you on this special day** to become:

 Thinking of you today and always

 b) Resize this text so that it fills most of the height of the artwork.

4 Draw a small **heart** shape with a solid **green** fill at the top right of the artwork to replace the deleted image.

5 a) Copy the small heart shape you drew in step 4.

 b) Move the copy so that it is positioned below the original as shown in **Build-up Task Layout Sketch 2**.

 c) Change the colour of the copied heart to **red**.

6 Save your artwork keeping the filename **gift**

7 Check your artwork to make sure that you have placed all items according to **Layout Sketch 2** and that you have carried out the 'Candidate instructions for the artwork'.

8 Print one copy of your artwork in colour.

9 On the printout write **your name**, **your centre number** and **the date** below the artwork.

10 Close all open files.

Before you begin this task make sure you have the following images:

○ a colour or black and white picture of card(s) for an occasion (e.g. birthday). The picture must be taken using a digital camera. If you do not have access to your own digital picture, you may use any one of the images **card1, card2 or card3** from the folder **files_imgcreation**

○ **march** from the folder **files_imgcreation**.

1   Open Photoshop.

2   **a)** Open the picture of card(s) for an occasion.
    b) Make sure your picture is not offensive, rude, inappropriate or unsuitable in any way.

3   **a)** Enter **your name** on the picture.
    b) You may position this text anywhere on the picture. Use a font colour and text size that will be clearly readable on the printout.

4   Save the picture using a suitable filename.

5   Print the picture in black and white.

6   Close the picture.

7   Open the image **march**.

You will need to change the resolution of the image **march** and take a screen print as evidence. You must keep the image approximately the same size (8 cm wide by 10.5 cm high).

8   **a)** Change the resolution of this image to be **20 pixels/cm** (or 50.8 pixels/inch).
    b) Take a screen print of the dialogue box showing the changed resolution.
    c) You may enter your name on the screen print document or handwrite it later.
    d) Save and print the screen print.

9   Save the changed image using the filename **daffy**

10 **a)** Print the image **daffy** in black and white.
    b) Make sure **your name** and **the date** are on all printouts.

11 Make sure you check all your printouts for accuracy.

12 Close the file and exit the software.

You should have the following printouts:
○ **card artwork** (in colour)
○ **gift artwork** (in colour)
○ **the digital picture of card(s) for an occasion** (in black and white)
○ **the screen print of the changed resolution** (in colour or black and white)
○ **daffy image** (in black and white)

Make sure your name is clearly displayed on all printouts.

Practice tasks

Candidate instructions for the artwork

All images:

- must not be distorted
- may be resized to suit the artwork
- must not touch or overlap any other items or the edge of the artwork.

All text:

- must not touch or overlap any other items or the edge of the artwork.

(Note that all items will be placed on the background layer)

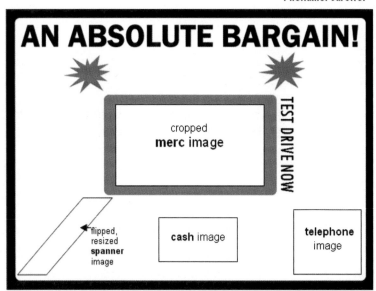

Practice Task Layout Sketch 1

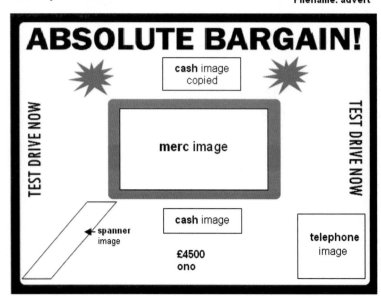

Practice Task Layout Sketch 2

Task 1

You will need the files **merc** and **telephone** from the folder **files_imgcreation**.

Refer to **Practice Task Layout Sketch 1** and the 'Candidate instructions for the artwork' on page 60.

1 a) Create a new piece of artwork which is **9.5 cm** wide by **7 cm** tall.
  b) Fill the background with **black**.

2 Draw a **white** rounded rectangle to fill most, but not all, of the space in the artwork. The black background of the artwork should display as a thick black outline around the white rectangle as shown on the layout sketch.

3 Draw a **red** rounded rectangle (approximately 4.5 cm wide by 2.5 cm tall) in the centre the artwork.

4 a) Open the image **merc**.
  b) Crop the image from all four directions to keep only the car. Do not cut out any part of the car.
  c) Insert the cropped image into the centre of the artwork to fit within the red rectangle as shown in **Practice Task Layout Sketch 1**. You may resize the image.

5 a) Enter the following text in **dark blue**:

  AN ABSOLUTE BARGAIN!

  b) Size this text to fill most of the width of the white rectangle.
  c) Position this text towards the top of the white rectangle.

6 a) Insert the image **telephone** at the bottom right corner of the white rectangle.
  b) Resize this image so that it is at least half its original size.

7 Save your artwork using the filename **caroffer**

Task 2

You will need the files **spanner** and **cash** from the folder **files_imgcreation**.

Refer to **Practice Task Layout Sketch 1** and the 'Candidate instructions for the artwork' on page 60.

Continue working on your artwork called **caroffer** that you saved in Task 1.

1 a) Enter the following text in **black**:

    TEST DRIVE NOW

  b) Rotate this text **90° clockwise (CW)**.
  c) Size the text so that it is approximately equal to the height of the red rectangle.
  d) Position this text as shown in **Practice Task Layout Sketch 1**.

2 a) Insert the image **spanner** at the bottom left of the white rectangle.
  b) **Flip** the spanner image **horizontally**.
  c) Resize this image so that it fits between the red and white rectangles.
  d) Move the image so that the jaw of the spanner (the 'U' shape) is positioned at the corner of the red rectangle.

3 a) Create a **green starburst** shape with a solid fill.
  b) Place this shape above the top left corner of the red rectangle.

4 a) Copy the green starburst shape.
  b) Position the copied shape above the top right corner of the red rectangle.

5 Insert the image **cash** in the bottom centre of the artwork.

6 Save your artwork keeping the filename **caroffer**.

7 Check your artwork to make sure that you have placed all items according to **Practice Task Layout Sketch 1** and that you have carried out the 'Candidate instructions for the artwork'.

8 Print your artwork in colour.

9 On the printout write **your name**, **your centre number** and **the date** anywhere below the artwork.

Task 3

Refer to **Practice Task Layout Sketch 2** and the 'Candidate instructions for the artwork' on page 60.

Continue working on your artwork called **caroffer** that you saved in Task 2.

1 Open your saved artwork **caroffer** (if it is not already open) and save it using the new filename **advert** as a Photoshop file.

2 Delete both the starburst shapes.

3 a) Amend the text **AN ABSOLUTE BARGAIN!** to become:

ABSOLUTE BARGAIN!

b) Resize this text so that it fills most of the width of the white rectangle.

4 a) Move the **cash** image further up as shown on Practice Task Layout Sketch 2.

b) Enter the following text in **dark green** on two lines below the **cash** image in the bottom centre of the artwork:

£4500

ono

5 a) Copy the text TEST DRIVE NOW
b) Rotate the copied text by **180˚**.
c) Position the copy to the left of the red rectangle at the edge of the white rectangle as shown in **Practice Task Layout Sketch 2**.

6 Move the original text to the right of the white rectangle as shown in **Practice Task Layout Sketch 2**.

7 a) Copy the **cash** image.
b) Position the copy above the red rectangle as shown in **Practice Task Layout Sketch 2**.
c) You may resize the copy if required.

8 Save your artwork keeping the filename **advert**

9 Check your artwork to make sure that you have placed all items according to **Practice Task Layout Sketch 2** and that you have carried out the 'Candidate instructions for the artwork'.

10 Print one copy of your artwork in colour.

11 On the printout write **your name**, **your centre number** and **the date** below the artwork.

12 Close all open files.

Task 4

Before you begin this task make sure you have the following images:

- a black and white picture of car(s). The picture must be taken using a digital camera. If you do not have access to your own digital picture, you may use any one of the images **car1, car2 or car3** from the folder **files_imgcreation**.
- **nocars** from the folder **files_imgcreation**.

1 Open Photoshop.

2 a) Open the picture of **car(s)**.

b) Make sure your picture is not offensive, rude, inappropriate or unsuitable in any way.

3 a) Enter **your name** on the picture.

b) You may position this text anywhere on the picture. Use a font colour and text size that will be clearly readable on the printout.

4 Save the picture using a suitable filename.

5 Print the picture in black and white.

6 Close the picture.

7 Open the image **nocars.jpg**.

You will need to change the resolution of the image **nocars** and take a screen print as evidence. You must keep the image **nocars** approximately the same size (17 cm wide by 15 cm high).

8 a) Change the resolution of the image to be **10 pixels/cm** (this is **25 pixels/inch**).

b) Take a screen print of the dialogue box showing the changed resolution.

c) You may enter your name on the screen print or handwrite it later.

d) Save and print the screen print.

9 Save the changed image using the filename **sign**

10 a) Print the image **sign**.

b) Write **your name** and **the date** on the printout.

11 Make sure you check all your printouts for accuracy.

12 Close the file and exit the software.

You should have the following printouts:
- **caroffer artwork** (in colour)
- **advert artwork** (in colour)
- **the digital picture of car(s)** (in black and white)
- **the screen print of the changed resolution** (in colour or black and white)
- **sign image** (in colour or black and white)

Make sure your name is clearly displayed on all printouts.

Refer to the handout on the accompanying CD-ROM for General assessment guidelines.

○ Your tutor will provide you with the file(s) supplied by OCR that you need for the assessment. In addition, you will also need a digital picture (refer to pages 45–47).

○ Before an assessment you should create a new folder just for the assessment.

TIP!

Before you start, **COPY** the folder containing the files into another user area in case you need to open an original file again. This is particularly important for this unit.

TASKS

There will usually be four tasks. The assignment will include two Layout Sketches and a section titled 'Candidate instructions for the completion of tasks'.

○ You will create a new piece of artwork to a specified size, fill the background with a colour and insert text and images.

○ You will then make changes to the artwork, e.g. edit text, move and/or copy images, delete an item. Both prints of the artwork will need to be printed in colour.

○ You will open an image provided by OCR and change the resolution.

○ You will open a picture that has been taken using a digital camera. This picture can be taken by yourself, your tutor or another tutor in your centre. You can enter your name anywhere on this image.

You will need to handwrite your name on the printouts of the artwork and the image with the amended resolution. You will enter your name on the digital picture.

Create a new piece of artwork

○ If possible, ask your tutor to photocopy the Layout Sketches on a separate sheet of paper on a single side.

○ Before you begin, detach the page with the Layout Sketches and keep this page next to your computer whilst you are producing the artwork.

○ Look at both Layout Sketches before you begin so that you have a visual picture of the artwork to be created and the amended artwork.

○ Do NOT attempt to create the artwork by referring only to the Layout Sketches. You must carry out the instructions in the order listed in the assignment.

○ The 'Candidate instructions for the completion of tasks' provided by OCR include an instruction that 'All images must have a transparent background (must allow the background color of the artwork to be seen)'. As you are using a professional Art package you do NOT need to make any changes to the transparency of any images. This instruction applies to those who may use non-Art packages.

○ The Photoshop settings on a particular computer will be those selected by the previous user (e.g. cm or inches, the resolution, the foreground color, the Toolbox tools, the palettes used). Therefore you are advised to use the technique you have learnt to restore the default settings before you begin an assessment.

- Make sure you check the unit of measurement is set to cm (centimetres) for both the height and the width.

- Photoshop will change the image size fractionally, e.g. 15cm would be resized to 14.99cm. You may notice this in the Print dialogue box. Do not be concerned, this is acceptable.

- The resolution for the artwork will not be specified in an OCR assignment, this is up to you. A standard screen resolution is 28.346 pixels/cm. Although this gives a reasonable image quality a higher resolution gives a better image quality. You are advised to set the resolution between 60 to 78 pixels/cm.

- Fit the artwork on screen so that it is clearer for you to see.

- In an OCR assignment, you will not be instructed to create a new layer for each item (image, block of text, shape). You are expected to know how to use the software. You must create a new layer for every image, phrase of text and for every shape.

- You are advised to give each layer a suitable name. However, if you have not done so, or made an error in a layer name during an assessment, do not spend too much time renaming layers, as the layer names are never displayed on any printout.

- If you need to crop an image, fit it on screen once you have opened it and before you crop so that it is clearer to see.

- You will not always be instructed to resize an image as you are expected to know which images should be resized. Refer to the Layout Sketch to help you see the *approximate* size of each image.

- Make sure you maintain the original proportion of all images. Do not distort the original shape when resizing or rotating images.

- When flipping an image the original size must be maintained. Photoshop does usually keep the original size when you flip.

- Once you have inserted images close the original images *without* saving any changes made to the original images.

- When drawing shapes, if the instruction is to draw a shape of an approximate size you may find it quicker to use the Fixed Size option in Photoshop and enter the width and height instead of trying to draw a freehand shape.

- Do refer to the Layout Sketch frequently. Try to draw shapes that are similar to those shown – the shapes do not have to be identical.

- You may use any legible font type and any emphasis (e.g. bold).

- Make sure that you fit the text as instructed. Remember, you can enter a font size with a decimal point if the size required is not displayed on the list.

- When instructed to rotate or flip an item (text, image or a shape) make sure you rotate or flip it in the direction specified. Mistakes can be made easily when rotating or flipping.

- Make sure you select the option to rotate to a set number of degrees (90 or 180). Do not select the free Rotate option.

- Use the **Ctrl** and **arrow** keys to position items more precisely.

- Although not essential, it is helpful to display the ruler and use ruler guides to help you position items.

- Zoom in on various parts of the artwork to make sure that items do not touch or overlap.

- Once you have printed you must check the printout to make sure that all colours have printed correctly. If the printer ink is low some colours may not print correctly. If this happens, tell your tutor. You can save the artwork and continue with the assessment, and print at another time.

- Make sure that all text is clearly readable on the printout.

- Write your first and last name on the printout above or below the artwork (and centre number and date if instructed).

Amend the artwork

- Before you begin a task, read through all the instructions. If you need to save the artwork with a different filename do so **before** you start the task. This will prevent accidentally saving over the original artwork.

- Refer to Layout Sketch 2 – keep this visible as you amend your artwork.

- When instructed to delete text, an image or a shape make sure you delete the entire layer.

- When instructed to copy an item, copy the entire layer.

- When you edit the text, make sure you size the amended text correctly. Even if there is no instruction that the font size should be amended, you are allowed to do so to help you fit the text.

Change the resolution

- When you open the image select the **Image** menu, then click **Image Size** and write down the size of the original image. It is also helpful to write down the original resolution.

- Next, change the measurement to **pixels/cm** (in an OCR assignment you will also be given the equivalent pixels/inch, you may use this instead).

- Then delete the existing figure for the resolution and enter the new figure. Do NOT click OK at this point as you will need to take a screen print.

- Press the Print Screen key to take a screen print. In Photoshop, do **not** press Alt + Print Screen because this resets any settings.

- Open Microsoft Word, paste the screen print, save it, print it and close Word. The **Image Size** dialogue box should still be displayed on the screen in Photoshop. Then click **OK** in the **Image Size** dialogue box.

- Do not be concerned if the image size becomes much smaller at this point. Use Fit on Screen to view the changed image. The quality of the image should be visibly different.

- Check the instructions to see if this image should be printed in colour or in black and white.

- Make absolutely sure that you save the image with the amended resolution using the new filename into your working folder. You should not save over the original image.

- Note that in the OCR Sample A assignment and some live assignments there is no instruction to take a screen print. This was introduced in Sample B.

Open a picture taken using a digital camera

- This picture is not provided by OCR. In each OCR assignment and on the 'Important notes for tutors' page which precedes the assignment, you and your tutor are told what the picture should be about.

- If you have access to a digital camera, or a mobile phone which takes digital pictures, you may take the picture yourself. You will then need to open the picture in Photoshop. You should practice this several times before beginning a live assessment.

- If you are taking the picture yourself your tutor should inform you before you begin the assessment what the picture should be of. You should take the picture and have it ready before you begin the assessment.

- Alternatively, a tutor may take the picture and provide it to you either on a digital memory card (this comes with a digital camera) or can give it to you along with the other files provided by OCR for the assessment.

- During the assessment all that you need to do is open the picture and type your name anywhere on top of the image in a place where your name can be easily read.

- You should then save the picture which includes your name and print it.

- Check the instructions to see if this image should be printed in colour or in black and white.

- Check all of your printouts for accuracy.

Good Luck!

Index